A voice said quietly, "Easy now, hands behind your neck and don't try anything stupid."

There was a soft footstep and the hard barrel of a gun was pushed against his back. As a hand reached for the hilt on the knife at his waist, he pivoted to the left, swinging away from the gunbarrel. There was a cry of dismay as their bodies came together and fell heavily to the floor. Chavasse raised his right arm to bring down the edge of his hand in the deadly karate blow that is as lethal as a woodman's axe. He paused.

For a moment she lay there, eyes widening in surprise, and then her hand reached for his.

"My name is Liri Kupi."

the keys of hell

jack higgins

FAWCETT GOLD MEDAL • NEW YORK

THE KEYS OF HELL

THIS BOOK CONTAINS THE COMPLETE TEXT OF
THE ORIGINAL HARDCOVER EDITION.

Published by Fawcett Gold Medal Books, a unit of CBS Publications, the Consumer Publishing Division of CBS Inc., by arrangement with Harold Ober Associates, Inc.

ISBN 0-449-13673-6

Printed in the United States of America

10 9 8 7 6 5 4

For Jan and Chris Hewitt,
who like a good story

There are no keys to Hell—the doors are open to all men.
                                         —Albanian proverb

the keys of hell

1

when in rome . . .

When Chavasse entered the Grand Ballroom of the British Embassy, he was surprised to find the Chinese delegation clustered around the fireplace, looking completely out of place in their blue uniforms, and surrounded by the cream of Roman society.

Chou En-lai surveyed the scene from a large gilt chair, the Ambassador and his wife beside him, and his smooth impassive face gave nothing away. Occasionally, guests of sufficient eminence were brought forward by the First Secretary to be introduced.

The orchestra was playing a waltz. Chavasse lit a cigarette and leaned against a pillar. It was a splendid scene, the crystal chandeliers taking light to every corner of the cream and gold ballroom, reflected again and again the mirrored walls.

Beautiful women, handsome men, dress uniforms, the scarlet and purple of church dignitaries—it was all strangely archaic as if somehow the mirrors were reflecting a dim memory of long ago, dancers turning endlessly to faint music.

He looked across to the Chinese and, for a brief instant, the white face of Chou En-lai seemed to jump out of the crowd, the eyes fastening on his. He nodded slightly as if they knew each other and the eyes seemed to say: *All these are doomed—this is my hour and you and I know it.*

Chavasse shivered and, for no accountable reason, a wave of greyness ran through him. It was as if some sixth sense, that mystical element common to all ancient races, inherited from his Breton father, were trying to warn him of danger.

The moment passed, the dancers swirled on. He was tired, that was the trouble. Four days on the run with no more than a couple of hours' uneasy sleep snatched when it was safe. He lit another cigarette and examined himself in the mirror on the wall.

The dark evening clothes were tailored to perfection, outlining good shoulders and a wiry muscular frame, but the skin was drawn too tightly over the high cheekbones that were a heritage from his French father, and there were dark circles under the eyes.

What you need is a drink, he told himself and, behind him in the mirror, a young girl came in from the terrace through the french windows.

Chavasse turned slowly. Her eyes were set too far apart, the mouth too generous. Her dark hair hung loosely to her shoulders and the white silk dress falling to just below the knee was simplicity itself. She wore no accessories. None were needed. Like all great beauties, she wasn't beautiful, but it didn't matter a damn. She made every other woman in the room seem insignificant.

She moved towards the bar, heads turning as she passed, and was immediately accosted by an Italian Air Force Colonel who was obviously slightly the worse for drink. Chavasse gave the man enough time to make a thorough nuisance of himself, then moved through the crowd to her side.

"Ah, there you are, darling," he said in Italian. "I've been looking everywhere for you."

Her reflexes were excellent. She turned smoothly, assessing him against the general situation in a split second and making her decision.

She reached up and kissed him lightly on the cheek. "You said you'd only be ten minutes. It's really too bad of you."

The Air Force Colonel had already faded discreetly into the crowd and Chavasse grinned. "How about a glass of Bolinger? I really think we should celebrate."

"I think that would be rather nice, Mr. Chavasse," she said in excellent English. "On the terrace, perhaps. It's cooler there."

Chavasse helped himself to two glasses of champagne from the table and followed her through the crowd, a slight frown on his face. It *was* cool on the terrace, the traffic sounds muted and far away and the scent of jasmine was heavy on the night air.

She sat on the balustrade and took a deep breath. "Isn't it a wonderful night?" She turned and looked at him and laughter bubbled out of her. "Francesca—Francesca Minetti."

She held out her hand and Chavasse gave her one of the glasses of champagne and grinned. "You seem to know who I am already."

She leaned back and looked up at the stars. When she spoke it was as if she were reciting a lesson hard-learned.

"Paul Chavasse, born Paris 1928, father French, mother English. Educated at Sorbonne, Cambridge and Harvard Universities. Ph.D. Modern Languages, multilingual. University lecturer until 1954. Since then . . ."

Her voice trailed away and she looked at him thoughtfully. Chavasse lit a cigarette, no longer tired. "Since then . . .?"

"Well, you're on the books as a Third Secretary, but you certainly don't look like one."

"What would you say I *did* look like?" he said calmly.

"Oh, I don't know. Someone who got about a lot." She swallowed some more champagne and said casually, "How was Albania? I was surprised you made it out in one piece. When the Tirana connection went dead we wrote you off."

She started to laugh again, her head back and behind Chavasse a voice said, "Is she giving you a hard time, Paul?"

Murchison, the First Secretary, limped across the terrace. He was a handsome, urbane man, face bronzed and healthy, the bar of medals a splash of bright colour on the left breast of his jacket.

"Let's say she knows rather too much about me for my personal peace of mind."

"Should do," Murchison said. "Francesca works for s2. She was your radio contact all last week. One of our best operatives."

Chavasse turned quickly. "You were the one who relayed the message from Scutari warning me to get out fast?"

She bowed. "Happy to be of service."

Before Chavasse could continue, Murchison took him firmly by the arm. "Now don't start getting emotional, Paul. Your boss has just got in and he wants to see you. You and Francesca can talk over old times later."

Chavasse grinned and squeezed her hand. "That's a promise. Don't go away."

"I'll wait right here," she assured him and he turned and followed Murchison inside.

They moved through the crowded ballroom into the entrance hall, passed the two uniformed footmen at the bottom of the grand staircase and mounted to the first floor.

The long, thickly carpeted corridor was quiet and the music, echoing from the ballroom, might have been from another world. They went up half a dozen steps, turned into a shorter side passage and paused outside a white-painted door.

"In here, old man," Murchison said. "Try not to be too long. We've a cabaret starting in half an hour. Really quite something, I promise you."

He moved back along the passage, his footsteps silent on the thick carpet and Chavasse knocked on the door, opened it and went in.

The room was a small plainly furnished office, its

walls painted a neutral shade of green. The young woman who sat at the desk writing busily was plump and attractive in spite of her dark, heavy-rimmed library spectacles.

She glanced up sharply and Chavasse grinned. "Surprise, surprise."

Jean Frazer removed her spectacles, a look of frank pleasure on her face. "You look like hell. How was Albania?"

"Tiresome," Chavasse said. "Cold, wet and with the benefits of universal brotherhood rather thinly spread on the ground." He sat on the edge of the desk and helped himself to a cigarette from a silver and teak box. "What brings you and the old man out here? The Albanian affair wasn't all that important."

"We had a NATO intelligence meeting in Bonn. When we got word that you were safely out, the Chief decided to come to Rome to take your report on the spot."

"Not good enough," Chavasse said. "The old bastard wouldn't have another job lined up for me, would he? Because if he has, he can damn well think again."

"Why not ask him?" she said. "He's waiting for you now."

She nodded towards a green baize door. Chavasse looked at it for a moment, sighed heavily and crushed his cigarette into the ashtray.

The inner room was half in shadow, the only light a shaded lamp on the desk. The man who stood at the window gazing out at the lights of Rome was of medium height, the face somehow ageless, a strange, brooding expression in the dark eyes.

"Here we are again," Chavasse said softly.

The Chief turned, the dark eyes taking in everything about Chavasse in a single moment. He nodded. "Glad to see you back in one piece, Paul. I hear things were pretty rough over there?"

"You could say that."

The older man moved to his chair and sat down. "Tell me about it."

"Albania?" Chavasse shrugged. "We're not going to do much there, I'm afraid. No one can pretend the people have gained anything since the Communists took over at the end of the war but there's no question of a counter revolution even getting started. The *sigurmi*, the secret police, are everywhere. I'd say they must be the most extensive in Europe."

"You went in using that Italian Communist Party Friendship cover, didn't you?"

"It didn't do me much good. The Italians in the party accepted me all right, but the trouble started when we reached Tirana. The *sigurmi* assigned an agent to each one of us personally and they were real pros. Shaking them was difficult enough and the moment I did, they smelt a rat and put out a general call for me."

"What about the Freedom Party? How extensive are they?"

"You can start using the past tense as of last week. When I arrived, they were down to two cells. One in Tirana, the capital, the other in Scutari. Both were still in contact with our s2 operation here in Rome."

"Did you manage to contact the leader, this man Luci?"

"Only just. The night we were to meet to really discuss things, he was mopped up by the *sigurmi*. Apparently, they were all over his place, waiting for me to show my hand."

"And how did you manage to scrape out of that one?"

"The Scutari cell got a radio signal from Luci as the police were breaking in. They relayed it to s2 Headquarters here in Rome. Luckily for me they had a quick thinker on duty—a girl called Francesca Minetti."

"One of our best people at this end," the Chief said. "I'll tell you about her one of these days."

"My back way out of Albania was a motor launch called *Buona Esperanza* run by a man called Guilio Orsini. He's quite a boy. Was one of the original torpedo merchants with the Italian Navy during the war. His best touch was when he sank a couple of our destroyers in Alexandria harbour back in '41. Got out again in one piece, too. He's a smuggler now. Runs across to Albania a lot. His grandmother came from there."

"As I recall the original plan, he was to wait three nights running in a cove near Durres. That's about thirty miles by road from Tirana, isn't it?"

Chavasse nodded. "When Francesca Minetti got the message from Scutari, she took a chance and put it through to Orsini on his boat. The madman left his crewman in charge, landed, stole a car in Durres and drove straight to Tirana. He caught me at my hotel as I was leaving for the meeting with Luci."

"Getting back to the coast must have been quite a trick."

"We did run into a little trouble. Had to do the last ten miles to the coast on foot. Once we were on board the *Buona Esperanza* it was easy. The Albanians don't have much of a navy. Half a dozen minesweepers and a couple of sub-chasers. The *Buona Esperanza* has ten knots on any one of them."

"It would seem that Orsini is due for a bonus on this one?"

"That's putting it mildly."

The Chief nodded, opened the official file which contained Chavasse's report and leafed through it. "So we're wasting our time in Albania?"

Chavasse nodded. "I'm afraid so. You know the way things have been since the 20th Party Congress in 1956 and now the Chinese are in there with both feet."

"Anything to worry about?"

Chavasse shook his head. "The most backward European country I've visited and the Chinese are too far from home to be able to do much about it."

"What about this naval base the Russians were using at Valona before they pulled out? The word was that they'd built it into a sort of Red Gibraltar on the Adriatic."

"Alb-Tourist took us on an official trip on our second day. Port is hardly the word for the place. Good natural shelter, but only used by fishing boats. Certainly no sign of submarine pens."

"And Enver Hoxha—you think he's still firmly in control?"

"And then some. We saw him at a military parade on the third day. He cuts an impressive figure, especially in uniform. He's certainly the people's hero at the moment. Heaven knows how long for."

The Chief closed the file with a quick gesture that somehow dismissed the whole affair, placing it firmly in the past.

"Good work, Paul. At least we know where we stand. Another piece in the jigsaw. You're due for some leave now, aren't you?"

"That's right," Chavasse said and waited.

The Chief got to his feet, walked to the window and looked out over the glittering city, down towards the Tiber. "What would you like to do?"

"Spend a week or two at Matano," Chavasse said without hesitation. "That's a small fishing port near Bari. There's a good beach and Guilio Orsini owns a place on the front called the *Tabu*. He's promised me some skin diving. I'm quite looking forward to it."

"I'm sure you are," the Chief said. "Sounds marvellous."

"Do I get it?"

The old man looked out over the city, an abstracted frown on his face. "Oh, yes, Paul, you can have your leave—after you've done a little chore for me."

Chavasse groaned and the older man turned and came back to the desk. "Don't worry, it won't take long, but you'll have to leave tonight."

"Is that necessary?"

The old man nodded. "I've got transport laid on

and you'll need help. Preferably this chap Orsini from
the sound of him. We'll offer a good price."

Chavasse sighed, thinking of Francesca Minetti
waiting on the terrace, of the good food and wine
in the buffet room below. He sighed again and stubbed
out his cigarette carefully.

"What do I do?"

The Chief pushed a file across. "Enrico Noci, a
double agent who's been working for us and the
Albanians. I didn't mind at first, but now the Chinese
have got to him."

"Which isn't healthy."

"They never are. Too damned earnest for my
liking. There's a boat waiting at Bari to take Noci
over to Albania tomorrow night. All the details are
in there."

Chavasse studied the picture, the heavy fleshy face,
the weak mouth. A man who was probably a failure
at everything he had put his hand to, except perhaps
women. He had the sort of tanned beach-boy good
looks that some of them went for.

"Do I bring him in?"

"What on earth for?" The Chief shook his head.
"Get rid of him; a swimming accident, anything you
like. Nothing messy."

"Of course," Chavasse said calmly.

He glanced through the file again, memorizing the
facts it contained, then pushed it across and stood up.
"I'll see you in London?"

The Chief nodded. "In three weeks, Paul. Enjoy
your holiday."

"Don't I always?"

The old man pulled a file across, opened it and started to study the contents and Chavasse crossed to the door and left quietly.

2

a fine night for dying

Enrico Noci lay staring through the darkness at the ceiling, smoking a cigarette. Beside him the woman slept, her thigh warm against his. Once, she stirred, turning into him in her sleep, but didn't awaken.

He reached for another cigarette and there was a slight distinctive rattle as something was pushed through the letter box in the outer hall. He slid from beneath the blankets, careful not to waken her and padded across the tiled floor in his bare feet.

A large buff envelope lay on the mat at the front door. He took it into the kitchen, lit the gas under the coffee pot and opened the envelope quickly. Inside there was a smaller sealed envelope, the one he was to take with him, and a single typed sheet containing his movement orders. He memorized them, then burned it quickly at the stove.

He glanced at his watch. Just before midnight.

Time for a hot bath and something to eat. He stretched lazily, a conscious pleasure seeping through him. The woman had really been quite something. Certainly a diverting way of spending his last evening.

He was wallowing up to his chin in hot water, the small bathroom half-full of steam when the door opened and she came in, yawning as she tied the belt of his silk dressing gown.

"Come back to bed, *caro*," she said plaintively.

For the life of him he couldn't remember her name and he grinned. "Another time, angel. I must get moving. Scrambled eggs and coffee like a good girl. I've got to be out of here in twenty minutes."

When he left the bathroom ten minutes later, he was freshly shaved, his dark hair slicked back and he wore an expensive hand-knitted sweater and slacks. She had laid a small table in the window and placed a plate of scrambled eggs in front of him as he sat down.

As he ate, he pulled back the curtain with one hand and looked down across the lights of Bari to the waterfront. The town was quiet and a slight rain drifted through the yellow street lamps in a silver spray.

"Will you be coming back?" she said.

"Who knows, angel?" he shrugged. "Who knows?"

He finished his coffee, went into the bedroom, picked up a dark blue nylon raincoat and a small canvas grip and returned to the living room. She sat with her elbows on the table, a cup of coffee in her hands. He took out his wallet, extracted a couple of banknotes and dropped them on the table.

"It's been fun, angel," he said and moved to the door.

"You know the address."

When he closed the outside door and turned along the street it was half past twelve exactly. The rain was falling quite heavily now and fog crouched at the ends of the streets, reducing visibility to thirty or forty yards.

He walked briskly along the wet pavement, turning confidently out of one street into another and, ten minutes later, halted beside a small black Fiat saloon. He opened the door, lifted the corner of the carpet and found the ignition key at once. A few moments later he was driving away.

On the outskirts of Bari, he stopped and consulted the map which he found in the glove compartment. Matano was about twelve miles away on the coast road running south to Brindisi. An easy enough run although the fog was bound to hold him up a little.

He lit a cigarette and started off again, concentrating on his driving as the fog grew thicker. He was finally reduced to a cautious crawl, his head out of the side window. It was almost an hour later when he halted at a signpost which indicated Matano to the left.

As he drove along the narrow road he could smell the sea through the fog and gradually it seemed to clear a little. He reached Matano fifteen minutes later and drove through silent streets towards the waterfront.

He parked the car in an alley near the *Club Tabu* as instructed and went the rest of the way on foot.

It was dark and lonely on the waterfront and the only sound was the lapping of water against the pilings as he went down a flight of stone steps to the jetty.

It was quiet and deserted in the yellow light of a solitary lamp and he paused half way along to examine the motor cruiser moored at the end. She was a thirty footer with a steel hull, probably built by Akerboon, he decided. She was in excellent trim, her sea-green paintwork gleaming. Not at all what he had expected. He examined the name *Buona Esperanza* on her counter with a slight frown.

When he stepped over the rail, the stern quarter was festooned with nets, still damp from the day's labour and stinking of fish, the deck slippery with their scales.

Somewhere in the distance the door of an all night café opened and music drifted out, faint and far away, and for no accountable reason Noci shivered. It was at that moment that he realized he was being watched.

The man was young, slim and wiry with a sun-blackened face that badly needed a shave. He wore denims and an old oilskin coat, and a seaman's cap shaded calm expressionless eyes. He stood at the corner of the deckhouse, a coiled rope in one hand and said nothing. As Noci took a step towards him, the door of the wheelhouse opened and another man appeared.

He was at least six feet three, great shoulders straining the seams of his blue pilot coat and wore an old Italian Navy officer's cap, the gold braid tarnished by exposure to salt air and water. He had perhaps the

ugliest face Noci had ever looked upon, the nose
smashed and flattened, the white line of an old scar
running from the right eye to the point of the chin.
A thin cigar of the type favoured by Dutch seamen
was firmly clenched between his teeth and he spoke
without removing it.

"Guilio Orsini, master of the *Buona Esperanza*."

Noci felt a sudden surge of relief flow through him
as tension ebbed away. "Enrico Noci."

He held out his hand. Orsini took it briefly and
nodded to the young deckhand. "Let's go, Carlo."
He jerked his thumb towards the companionway.
"You'll find a drink in the saloon. Don't come up
till I tell you."

As Noci moved towards the companionway, Carlo
cast off and moved quickly to the stern. The engine
burst into life, shattering the quiet and the *Buona
Esperanza* turned from the jetty and moved into the
fog.

The saloon was warm and pleasantly furnished.
Noci looked around approvingly, placed his canvas
grip on the table and helped himself to a large whisky
from a cabinet in one corner. He drank it quickly
and lay on one of the bunks smoking a cigarette, a
warm, pleasurable glow seeping through him.

This was certainly an improvement on the old tub
in which he had done the run to Albania before.
Orsini was a new face, but then there was nothing
surprising in that. The faces changed constantly. In
this business it didn't pay to take chances.

The boat lifted forward with a great surge of power
and a slight smile of satisfaction touched Noci's

mouth. At this rate they would be landing him on the coast near Durres before dawn. By noon he would be in Tirana. Another five thousand dollars to his account in the Bank of Geneva and this was his sixth trip in as many months. Not bad going, but you could take the pitcher to the well too often. After this a rest was indicated—a long rest.

He decided he would go to the Bahamas. White beaches, blue skies and a lovely tanned girl wading thigh deep from the sea to meet him. American for preference. They were so ingenuous, had so much to learn.

The engines coughed once and died away and *Buona Esperanza* slowed violently as her prow sank into the waves. Noci sat up, head to one side as he listened. The only sound was the lapping of the water against her hull.

It was some sixth sense, product of his years of treachery and double dealing, of living on his wits, that warned him that something was wrong. He swung his legs to the floor, reached for the canvas grip, unzipped it and took out a Biretta. He released the safety catch and padded across to the foot of the companionway. Above him, the door opened and shut, creaking slightly as the boat pitched in the swell.

He went up quickly, one hand against the wall, paused, and raised his head cautiously. The deck seemed deserted, the drizzle falling in silver cobwebs through the navigation lights.

He stepped out and, on his right, a match flared and a man moved out of the shadows, bending his head to light a cigarette. The flame revealed a handsome, devil's face, eyes like black holes above high cheekbones. He flicked the match away and stood there, hands in the pockets of his slacks. He wore a heavy fisherman's sweater and his dark hair glistened with moisture.

"Signor Noci?" he said calmly in fluent Italian.

"Who the hell are you?" Noci demanded and a cold finger moved inside him.

"My name is Chavasse—Paul Chavasse."

It was a name Noci was completely familiar with. An involuntary gasp rose in his throat and he raised the Biretta. A hand like iron clamped on his wrist, wrenching the weapon from his grasp and Guilio Orsini said, "I think not."

Carlo moved out of the shadows to the left and stood waiting. Noci looked about him helplessly and Chavasse held out his hand.

"I'll have the envelope now."

Noci produced it reluctantly and handed it across, trying to stay calm as Chavasse examined the contents. They could be no more than half a mile from the shore, no distance to a man who had been swimming since childhood and Noci was under no illusions as to what would happen if he stayed.

Chavasse turned over the first sheet of paper and Noci ducked under Orsini's arm and ran for the stern rail. He was aware of a sudden cry, an unfamiliar voice, obviously Carlo's, and then he slipped on some fish scales and stumbled headlong into the draped nets.

He tried to scramble to his feet, a foot tripped him and then the soft clinging, stinking meshes seemed to wrap themselves around him. He was pulled forward on to his hands and knees and looked up through the mesh to see Chavasse peering down at him, the devil's face calm and cold.

Orsini and Carlos had a rope in their hands and, in that terrible moment, Noci realized what they intended to do and the scream rose in his throat.

Orsini pulled hard on the rope and Noci lurched across the deck and cannoned into the low rail. A foot caught him hard against the small of the back and he went over into the cold water.

As he surfaced, the net impeding every movement he tried to make, he was aware of Orsini running the end of the line around the rail, of Carlo leaning out of the wheelhouse window waiting. A hand went up, the *Buona Esperanza* surged forward.

Noci went under with a cry, surfaced on a wave, choking for breath. He was aware only of Chavasse at the rail watching, face calm in the fog-shrouded light and then, as the boat increased speed, he went under for the last time.

As he struggled violently, water forcing the air from his lungs, he was aware of no pain, no pain at all. He seemed to be floating on soft white sand beneath a blue sky and a beautiful sun-tanned girl waded from the sea to join him and she was smiling.

3

the virgin of scutari

Chavasse was tired and his throat was raw from too many cigarettes. Smoke hung in layers from the low ceiling, spiralling in the heat from the single bulb above the green baize table, drifting into the shadows.

There were half a dozen men sitting in on the game. Chavasse, Orsini, Carlo Arezzi, his deckhand, a couple of fishing boat captains and the sergeant of police. Orsini lit another of his foul smelling Dutch cheroots and pushed a further two chips into the centre.

Chavasse shook his head and tossed in his hand. "Too rich for my blood, Guilio."

There was a general murmur and Guilio Orsini grinned and raked in his winnings. "Bluff, Paul, always the big bluff. That's all that counts in this game."

Chavasse wondered if that explained why he was so bad at cards. For him, action had to be part of a

logical progression from a carefully reasoned calcula-
tion of the risk involved. In the great game of life
and death he had played for so long, a man could
seldom bluff more than once and get away with it.

He pushed back his chair and stood up. "That's
me for tonight, Guilio. I'll see you on the jetty in
the morning."

Orsini nodded. "Seven sharp, Paul. Maybe we'll
get you that big one."

The cards were already on their way round again
as Chavasse crossed to the door, opened it and stepped
into a whitewashed passage. In spite of the lateness
of the hour, he could hear music from the front of
the club and careless laughter. He took down an old
reefer jacket from a peg, pulled it on and opened the
side door.

The cold night air cut into his lungs as he breathed
deeply to clear his head and moved along the alley.
A thin sea fog rolled in from the water and, except
for the faint strains of music from the *Tabu*, silence
reigned.

He found a crumpled packet of cigarettes in his
pocket, extracted one and struck a match on the
wall, momentarily illuminating his face. A woman
emerged from a narrow alley opposite, hesitated, then
walked down towards the jetty, the clicking of her
high heels echoing through the night. A moment later,
two sailors moved out of the entrance of the *Tabu*,
crossed in front of Chavasse and followed her.

Chavasse leaned against the wall feeling curiously
depressed. There were times when he really wondered
what it was all about, not just this dangerous game

he played, but life itself. He smiled in the darkness. Three o'clock in the morning on the waterfront of any kind of port was one hell of a time to start thinking like that.

The woman screamed and he flicked his cigarette into the fog and stood listening. Again the screaming sounded, curiously muffled, and he started to run towards the jetty. He turned a corner and found the two sailors holding her on the ground under a street lamp.

As the nearest one turned in alarm, Chavasse lifted a boot into his face and sent him back over the jetty. The other leapt towards him with a curse, steel glinting in his right hand.

Chavasse was aware of the black beard, blazing eyes and strange hooked scar on the right cheek and then he flicked his cap into the man's face and raised a knee into the exposed groin. The man writhed on the ground, gasping for breath and Chavasse measured the distance and kicked him in the head.

In the water below the jetty there was a violent splashing and he moved to the edge and saw the first man swimming vigorously into the darkness. Chavasse watched him disappear, then turned to look for the woman.

She was standing in the shadow of a doorway and he went towards her. "Are you all right?"

"I think so," she replied in a strangely familiar voice and stepped out of the shadows.

His eyes widened in amazement. "Francesca—Francesca Minetti. What in the world are you doing here?"

Her dress had been ripped from neck to waist and she held it in place, a slight smile on her face. "We were supposed to have a date on the terrace at the Embassy a week ago. What happened?"

"Something came up," he said. "The story of my life. But what are you doing on the Matano waterfront at this time of the morning?"

She swayed forward and he caught her just in time, holding her close to his chest for a brief moment. She smiled up at him wanly.

"Sorry about that, but all of a sudden I felt a little light-headed."

"Have you far to go?"

She brushed a tendril of hair back from her forehead. "I left my car somewhere near here, but all the streets look the same in the fog."

"Better come back with me to my hotel," he said. "It's just around the corner." He slipped off his jacket and draped it round her shoulders. "I could probably fix you up with a bed."

Laughter bubbled out of her and for a moment she was once again the gay exciting girl he had met so briefly at the Embassy ball.

"I'm sure you could."

He grinned and put an arm round her. "I think you've had quite enough excitement for one night."

There was the scrape of a shoe on the cobbles behind them and he swung round and saw the other man lurching into the fog, hands to his smashed face.

Chavasse took a quick step after him and Francesca caught his sleeve. "Let him go. I don't want the police in on this."

He looked down into her strained and anxious face, frowning slightly. "All right, Francesca. If that's the way you want it."

There was something strange here, something he didn't understand. They walked along the jetty and turned on to the waterfront. As port towns went Matano was reasonably tame, but not so tame that pretty young girls could walk around the dock area at three a.m. and expect to get away with it. One thing was certain. Francesca Minetti must have had a pretty powerful reason for being there.

The hotel was a small stuccoed building on a corner, an ancient electric sign over the entrance, but it was clean and cheap and the food was good. The owner was a friend of Orsini.

He slept at the desk, head in hands, and Chavasse reached over to the board without waking him and unhooked the key. They crossed the hall, mounted narrow wooden stairs and passed along a whitewashed corridor.

The room was plainly furnished with a brass bed, a washstand and an old wardrobe. As elsewhere in the house, the walls were whitewashed and the floor highly polished.

Francesca stood just inside the door, one hand to the neck of her dress, holding it in place and looked around approvingly.

"This is nice. Have you been here long?"

"Almost a week now. My first holiday in a year or more."

He opened the wardrobe, rummaged among his clothes and finally produced a black polo neck sweater in merino wool. "Try that for size while I get you a drink. You look as if you could do with one."

She turned her back and pulled the sweater over her head as he went to a cupboard in the corner. He took out a bottle of whisky and rinsed a couple of glasses in the bowl on the washstand. When he turned she was standing by the bed watching him, looking strangely young and defenceless, the dark sweater hanging loosely about her.

"Sit down, for God's sake, before you fall down," he said.

There was a cane chair by the french window leading to the balcony and she slumped into it and leaned her head against the glass window, staring into the darkness. Out at sea, a foghorn boomed eerily and she shivered.

"I think that must be the loneliest sound in the world."

"Thomas Wolfe preferred a train whistle," Chavasse said, pouring whisky into one of the glasses and handing it to her.

She looked puzzled. "Thomas Wolfe? Who was he?"

He shrugged. "Just a writer—a man who knew what loneliness was all about." He swallowed a little of his whisky. "Girls like you shouldn't be on the waterfront at this time of the morning, I suppose you know that? If I hadn't arrived when I did, you'd have probably ended up in the water after they'd finished with you."

She shook her head. "It wasn't that kind of assault."

"I see." He drank some more of his whisky and

considered the point. "If it would help, I'm a good listener."

She held her glass in both hands and stared down at it, a troubled look on her face, and he added gently, "Is this something official? An s2 operation, perhaps?"

She looked up, real alarm on her face and shook her head vigorously. "No, they know nothing about it and they mustn't be told, you must promise me that. It's a family matter, quite private."

She put down her glass, stood up and walked restlessly across the room. When she turned, there was an expression of real anguish on her face. She pushed her hair back with a quick nervous gesture and laughed.

"The trouble is, I've always worked inside. Never in the field. I just don't know what to do in a situation like this."

Chavasse produced his cigarettes, put one in his mouth and tossed the packet across to her. "Why not tell me about it? I'm a great one for pretty girls in distress."

She caught the packet automatically and stood there looking at him, a slight frown on her face. She nodded slowly. "All right, Paul, but anything I tell you is confidential. I don't want any of this getting back to my superiors at s2. It could get me into real trouble."

"Agreed," he said.

She came back to her chair, took a cigarette from the packet and reached up for a light. "How much do you know about me, Paul?"

He shrugged. "You work for s2 in Rome. My own boss told me you were one of the best people we had out here and that's good enough for me."

"I've worked for s2 for two years now," she said. "My mother was Albanian, so I speak the language fluently. I suppose that's what first interested them in me. She was the daughter of a *gegh* chieftain. My father was a colonel of mountain troops in the Italian occupation army in 1939. He was killed in the Western Desert early in the war."

"Is your mother still alive?"

"She died about five years ago. She was never able to return to Albania once Enver Hoxha and the Communists took over. Two of her brothers were members of the *Legaliteri* in North Albania which had royalist aims. They fought with Abas Kupi during the war. In 1945 Hoxha called them in from the hills to a peace conference at which they were immediately executed."

There was no pain on her face, no emotion at all, except a calm acceptance of what must have been for a long time quite simply a fact of life.

"At least that explains why you were willing to work for s2," Chavasse said softly.

"It was not a hard decision to make. There was only an old uncle, my father's brother, who raised us, and until last year my brother was still in Paris studying political economy at the Sorbonne."

"Where is he now?"

"When I last saw him, he was face down in a mud bank of the Buene Marshes in Northern Albania with a machine gun burst in his back."

Out of the silence, Chavasse said carefully, "When was this?"

"Three months ago. I was on leave at the time." She held out her glass. "Could I have some more?"

He poured until she raised her hand. She sipped a little, apparently still perfectly in control of her emotions and continued.

"You were in Albania not so long ago yourself. You know how things are."

He nodded. "As bad as I've seen."

"Did you notice any churches on your travels?"

"One or two still seemed to be functioning, but I know the official party line is to clamp down on religious observances of any sort."

"They've almost completely crushed Islam," she said in a dry matter of fact voice. "The Albanian Orthodox Church has come out of it a little better because they deposed their Archbishop and put in a priest loyal to Communism. It's the Roman Catholic Church which has been the most harshly persecuted."

"A familiar pattern," Chavasse said. "The organization Communism fears most."

"Out of two archbishops and four bishops arrested, two have been shot and another's on the books as having died in prison. The Church has almost ceased to exist in Albania, or so the authorities hoped."

"I must admit that was the impression I got."

"During the past year there's been an amazing revival in the north," she said. "Headed by the Franciscan fathers at Scutari. Even non-Catholics have been swarming into the church there. It's had the central government in Tirana quite worried. They decided to do something about it. Something spectacular."

"Such as?"

"There's a famous shrine outside the city dedicated to Our Lady of Scutari. A grotto and medicinal spring. The usual sort of thing. A place of pilgrimage since the Crusades. The statue is ebony and leafed with gold. Very ancient. They call her the Black Madonna. It's traditionally said that it was only because of her miraculous powers that the Turkish overlords of ancient times allowed Christianity to survive at all in the country."

"What did the central government intend to do?"

"Destroy the shrine, seize the statue and burn it publicly in the main square at Scutari. The Franciscan fathers were warned and managed to spirit the Madonna away on the very day the authorities were going to act."

"Where is it now?"

"Somewhere in the Buene Marshes at the bottom of a lagoon in my brother's launch."

"What happened?"

"It's easily told." She shrugged. "Marco was interested in a society of Albanian refugees living in Taranto. One of them, a man called Ramiz, got word about the Madonna through a cousin living in Albania at Tama. That's a small town on the river ten miles inland."

"And they decided to go in and bring her out?"

"The Black Madonna is no ordinary statue, Paul," she said seriously. "She symbolizes all the hope that's left for Albania in a hard world. They realized what a tremendous psychological effect it would have upon the morale of Albanians everywhere if it were made public in the Italian press that the statue had reached Italy in safety."

"And you went in with them?"

"It's an easy passage and the Albanian Navy is extremely weak so getting into the marshes is no problem. We picked up the statue at a prearranged spot on the first night. Unfortunately, we ran into a patrol boat next morning on the way out. There was some shooting and the launch was badly damaged. She sank in a small lagoon and we took to the rubber dinghy. They hunted us for most of the day. Marco was shot towards evening. I didn't want to leave his body, but we didn't have much choice. Later that night, we reached the coast and Ramiz stole a small sailing boat. That's how we got back."

"And where is this man Ramiz now?" Chavasse asked.

"Somewhere in Matano. He telephoned me in Rome yesterday and told me to meet him at a hotel on the waterfront. You see, he's managed to get hold of a launch."

Chavasse stared at her, an incredulous frown on his face. "Are you trying to tell me you intend to go back into those damned marshes?"

"That was the general idea."

"Just the two of you, you and Ramiz?" He shook his head. "You wouldn't last five minutes."

"Perhaps not, but it's worth a try." He started to protest and she raised a hand. "I'm not going to spend the rest of my life living with the thought that my brother died for nothing when I could at least have tried to do something about it. The Minettis are a proud family, Paul. We take care of our dead. I know what Marco would have done and I am the only one left to do it."

She sat there, proud and beautiful, her face very pale in the lamplight. Chavasse took her hands, reached across and kissed her gently on the mouth.

"This lagoon where the launch sank, you know where it is?"

She nodded, frowning slightly. "Why?"

He grinned. "You surely didn't think I intended to let you go in on your own?"

There was a look of complete bewilderment on her face. "But why, Paul? Give me one good reason why you should risk your life for me?"

"Let's just say I'm bored stiff after a week of lazing around on the beach and leave it at that. This man Ramiz, you've got his address?"

She took a scrap of paper from her handbag and handed it to him. "I don't think it's far from here."

He slipped it into his pocket. "Right, let's get going."

"To see Ramiz?"

He shook his head. "That comes later. First we'll call on a good friend of mine, the kind of friend you need for a job like this. Someone with no scruples, who knows the Albanian coast like the back of his hand and runs the fastest boat in the Adriatic."

At the door, she turned, looked up at him searchingly. Something glowed in her eyes and colour flooded her cheeks. Quite suddenly, she seemed confident, sure of herself again.

"It's going to be all right, angel. I promise you."

He raised her hand briefly to his lips, opened the door and gently pushed her into the corridor.

the smell of blood

The air in the room was still heavily tainted by cigarette smoke, but the card players had gone. In the light of the shaded lamp, a British Admiralty chart of the Drin Gulf area of the Albanian coast was unfolded across the table. Chavasse and Orsini leaned over it and Francesca sat beside them.

"The Buene River runs down to the coast from Lake Scutari or Shkoder as they call it these days," Orsini said.

"What about these coastal marshes? Are they as bad as Francésca says?"

Orsini nodded. "One hell of a place. A maze of narrow channels, salt-water lagoons and malaria-infested swamps. Unless you knew where to look, you could search for a year for that launch and never find it."

"Anyone living there?"

"A few fishermen and wildfowlers, mainly *geghs*. The Reds haven't done too well in those parts. The whole area's always been a sort of refuge for people on the run."

"You know it well?"

Orsini grinned. "I'd say I've made the run into those marshes at least half a dozen times this year. Penicillin, sulphonamide, guns, nylons. There's a lot of money to be made and the Albanian Navy can't do much to stop it."

"Still a risky business, though."

"For amateurs, anything is risky." Orsini turned to Francesca. "This man Ramiz, what did he do for a living?"

"He was an artist. I believe he did most of his sailing at weekends."

Orsini looked at the ceiling and raised his hands helplessly. "My God, what a set-up. That he got you back safely to Italy is a miracle, *signorina*."

The door opened and Carlo came in carrying several cups on a tray. He handed them round and Chavasse sipped hot coffee gratefully. He frowned down at the map, following the main channel, then turned to Francesca.

"You say you know where the launch went down? How can you be sure? These lagoons all look the same."

"Marco took a cross bearing just before we sank," she said. "I memorized it."

Orsini pushed a piece of paper and a pencil across and she quickly wrote the figures down. He examined them with a slight frown and then calculated the

position with infinite care. He drew a circle round
the central point, straightened and grinned.

"X marks the spot."

Chavasse examined it quickly. "About five miles in.
Another three or four to this place Tama. What's it
like there?"

"Used to be quite a thriving little river port years
ago, but it's gone down the slot in a big way since
the trouble started between Albania and the satellite
countries." Orsini traced a finger along the line of
the river. "The Buene forms part of the boundary
between Albania and Yugoslavia. Most of the main
stream's been allowed to silt up. That means you
have to know the estuary and delta region well to
get as far inland as Tama."

"But could you get us there?"

Orsini turned to Carlo. "What do you think?"

"We've never had any trouble before. Why should
we now?"

"The pitcher can go to the well too often," Francesca observed softly.

Orsini shrugged. "For all men, death makes the
last appointment. He chooses his own time."

"That only leaves the question of the price to be
settled," Chavasse said.

"No problem there," Francesca put in quickly.

"*Signorina*, please." Orsini took her hand and
touched it to his lips. "This thing I will do because
I want to and for no other reason."

She seemed close to tears and Chavasse interrupted
quickly. "One thing I'm not happy about is Ramiz.
Are you sure it was his voice on the telephone?"

She nodded. "He came from the province of Vlore. They have a distinctive accent. I'm sure it was him."

Chavasse decided that it didn't look too good for Ramiz. Quite obviously the *sigurmi* had traced them with no difficulty. Maybe they'd recovered Marco Minetti's body or what was more probable, had got their hands on the people who had passed on the Madonna in Albania itself. Each man had his limits, his specific tolerance to pain. Once past that point, most would babble all they knew before dying.

And it was natural that the Albanians should go to so much trouble to trace the Madonna. Its disappearance must have meant a big loss of prestige politically and the knowledge that it must still be in their own territory would be an added spur to recover it.

"If Ramiz did make that phone call it was probably because he was made to. Either that or he was known to have made it." He produced the slip of paper Francesca had given him at the hotel. "Do you know this place?"

Orsini nodded. "It's not far from here. The sort of fleabag where whores rent rooms by the hour and no questions asked." He turned to Francesca. "No place for a lady."

She started to protest, but Chavasse cut in quickly. "Guilio's right. In any case, you're out on your feet. What you need is about eight hours' solid sleep. You can use my room at the hotel." He turned to Carlo. "See she gets there safely."

He pulled on his reefer jacket and she stood up. "You'll be careful?"

"Aren't I always?" He gave her a little push. "Lock yourself in the room and get some sleep. I'll be along later."

She went reluctantly and Carlo followed her out. When Chavasse turned, Orsini was grinning hugely. "Ah, to be young and handsome."

"Something you never were," Chavasse said. "Let's get moving."

It was still raining, a thin drizzle that beaded the iron railings of the harbour wall like silver as they walked along the pavement. The old stuccoed houses floated out of the fog, unreal and insubstantial, and each street lamp was a yellow oasis of light in a dark world.

The hotel was no more than five minutes from the *Tabu*, a seedy tenement, plaster peeling from the brickwork beside the open door. They entered a dark and gloomy hall. There was no one behind the wooden desk and no response to Orsini's impatient push on the bell.

"Did she give you the room number?"

Chavasse nodded. "Twenty-six."

The Italian moved behind the desk and examined the board. He came back, shaking his head. "The key isn't there. He must still be in his room."

They went up a flight of rickety wooden stairs to the first floor. There was an unpleasant musty smell compounded of cooking odours and stale urine and a strange brooding quiet. They moved along the passage, checking the numbers on the doors and Chavasse became aware of music and high brittle laughter.

He paused outside the room from which it came and Orsini turned from the door opposite.

"This is it."

The door swung open to his touch and he stepped inside and reached for the light switch. Nothing happened. He struck a match and Chavasse moved in beside him.

The room was almost bare. There was a rush mat on the floor, an iron bed and a washstand. A wooden chair lay on its side beside the mat.

As Chavasse reached down to pick it up, the match Orsini was holding burned his fingers and he dropped it with a curse. Chavasse rested on one knee, waiting for him to light another and was aware of a sudden dampness soaking through the knee of his slacks. As the match flared, he raised his hand, the fingers sticky and glutinous with half-dried blood.

"So much for Ramiz."

They examined the room quickly but there was nothing to be found, not even a suitcase, and they went back into the passage. High pitched laughter sounded from opposite and Orsini raised his eyebrows enquiringly.

"Nothing to lose," Chavasse said.

The big Italian knocked on the door. There was a sudden silence and then a woman's voice called, "Come back later. I'm busy."

Orsini knocked even harder. There was a quick angry movement inside and the door was jerked open. The woman who faced them was small and fat with flaming red hair. The black nylon robe she wore did little to conceal her ample charms. She obviously recognized Orsini immediately and the look of anger on her face was replaced by a ready smile.

"Eh, Guilio, it's been a long time."

"Too long, *cara*," he said, patting her face. "You still look as good as ever. My friend and I wanted a word with the man opposite, but he doesn't appear to be at home."

"Oh, that one," she said in obvious disgust. "Sitting around his room like that. Wouldn't even give a girl the time of day."

"He must have been blind," Orsini said gallantly.

"A couple of men came looking for him earlier," she said. "I think there was some trouble. When I looked out, they were taking him away between them. He didn't look too good."

"You didn't think of calling the police?" Chavasse asked.

"I wouldn't cut that bastard of a sergeant down if he were hanging." There was an angry call from inside the room and she grinned. "Some of them get really impatient."

"I bet they do," Chavasse said.

She smiled. "You, I definitely like. Bring him round some time, Guilio. We'll have ourselves a party."

"Maybe I'll do that," Orsini told her.

There was another impatient cry from inside and she raised her eyebrows despairingly and closed the door.

Orsini and Chavasse went back downstairs and out into the street. The Italian paused to light a cheroot and flicked the match into the darkness.

"What now?"

Chavasse shrugged. "There isn't really much we can do. I know one thing. I could do with some sleep."

Orsini nodded. "Go back to your hotel. Stay with the girl and behave yourself. We'll sort something out in the morning." He punched Chavasse lightly on the shoulder. "Don't worry, Paul. You're in the hands of experts."

He turned away into the fog and as Chavasse watched him go tiredness seemed to wash over him in a great wave. He walked along the pavement, footsteps echoing between narrow stone walls and paused on a corner, fumbling for a cigarette.

As the match flared in his hands, something needle sharp sliced through his jacket to touch his spine. A voice said quietly, "Please to stand very still, Mr. Chavasse."

He waited while the expert hands passed over his body, checking for the weapon that wasn't there.

"Now walk straight ahead and don't look round. And do exactly as you are told. It would desolate me to have to kill you."

It was only as he started walking that the realization hit Chavasse with the force of a physical blow. The voice had spoken in Albanian.

5

the man from alb-tourist

There were two of them, he could tell that much from their footfalls echoing between the walls of the narrow alleys as they moved through the old quarter of the town. The harsh voice of the man who had first spoken occasionally broke the silence to tell him to turn right or left, but otherwise there was no conversation and they stayed well behind him.

Fifteen minutes later, they emerged from an alley on to the sea wall on the far side of the harbour from the jetty. An old house several floors high reared into the night and beside it, a flight of stone steps led down to a landing stage.

An old naval patrol boat was moored there, shabby and neglected, paint peeling from her hull. Across her stern ran the faded inscription *Stromboli—Taranto*.

The landing stage was deserted in the light of a

solitary lamp and there was no one to help him. He turned slowly and faced the two men. One of them was small and rather nondescript. He wore a heavy jersey and a knitted cap was pulled over his eyes.

The other was a different proposition, a big, dangerous looking man badly in need of a shave. He had a scarred, brutal face, cropped hair and wore a reefer coat and seaboots.

He slipped a cigarette into his mouth and struck a match on the seawall. "Down we go, Mr. Chavasse. Down we go."

Chavasse descended the steps slowly. As he reached the landing stage, the little man moved past him and led the way to the far end where he opened a door set in the thickness of the wall. A flight of stone stairs lifted into the gloom and Chavasse followed him, the big man a couple of paces behind.

They arrived on a stone landing and the little man opened another door and jerked his head. Chavasse moved past him and stood just inside the entrance. The room was plainly furnished with a wooden table and several chairs. A narrow iron bed stood against one wall.

The man who sat at the table writing a letter was small and dark and impeccably dressed in a suit of blue tropical worsted. His skin was the colour of fine leather, the narrow fringe of beard combining to give him the look of a *conquistadore*.

Chavasse paused a couple of feet away, hands in pockets. Small, black, shining eyes had swivelled to a position from which they could observe him. The man half-turned and smiled charmingly.

"Mr. Chavasse—a distinct pleasure, sir."

His English was clipped and precise, hardly any accent at all. Chavasse decided that he didn't like him. The eyes were cold and merciless in spite of the polite, bird-like expression, the eyes of a killer.

"I'm beginning to find all this rather a bore," he said.

The little man smiled. "Then we must try to make things more interesting. How would you like to earn ten thousand pounds?"

At the other end of the table was a tray containing a couple of bottles and several glasses. Chavasse walked to it calmly, aware of a slight movement from the big man over by the door.

One of the bottles contained Smirnoff, his favourite vodka. He half-filled a glass and walked casually to the window, gazing forty feet down into the harbour as he drank, assessing the position of the *Stromboli* to the left, her outline showing dimly through the fog.

"Well?" the little man asked.

Chavasse turned. "How are things in Tirana these days?"

The little man smiled. "Very astute, but I haven't seen Tirana in five years. A slight difference of opinion with the present regime." He produced a white card and flicked it across. "My card, sir. I am Adem Kapo, agent for Alb-Tourist in Taranto."

"Among other things, I'm sure."

Kapo took out a case and extracted a cigarette which he fitted into a holder. "You could describe me as a sort of middle-man. People come to me with their requirements and I try to satisfy them."

"For a fee?"

"But of course." He extended the case. "Cigarette?"

Chavasse took one. "Ten thousand pounds. That's a lot of money. What makes you think I'd be interested?"

"Knowing who people are is part of my business and I know a great deal about you, my friend. More than you could dream of. Men like you are a gun that is for sale to the highest bidder. In any case, the money would be easily earned. My principals will pay such a sum in advance if you will agree to lead them to the position of a certain launch which recently sank in the marshes of the Bucne River in Northern Albania. You are interested?"

"I could be if I knew what you were talking about."

"I'm sure Signorina Minetti has already filled you in on the details. Come now, Mr. Chavasse, all is discovered, as they say in the English melodramas. According to the information supplied to me by my clients, the body of an Italian citizen, one Marco Minetti, was discovered on a mud bank at the mouth of the Buene recently after an attempt had been made to smuggle a priceless religious relic from the country."

"You don't say," Chavasse said.

Kapo ignored the interruption. "A few hours earlier his launch had disappeared into the wastes of the Buene Marshes. Later, a priest and two men were taken into custody by the *sigurmi* at the town of Tama. Apparently, the priest was stubborn to the end, a bad habit they have, but the two men talked. They named Minetti, his sister and an Albanian refugee, an artist called Ramiz. I was offered what I must admit was a very handsome fee to trace them."

"And did you?"

"We've been watching Ramiz for weeks, waiting for him to make his move. Incredible though it may seem, he apparently intended to go in again. You see, he was an intellectual—one of those rather irritating people who feel they have a mission in life."

"You speak of him in the past tense?"

"Yes, it's really quite sad." Kapo sounded genuinely moved. "I decided to have a little chat with him earlier this evening. When Haji and Tasko were bringing him here, there was some sort of struggle. He fell from the seawall and broke his neck."

"Just an unfortunate accident, I suppose?"

"But of course, and quite unnecessary. It's surprising how easily one's motives can be misunderstood. I'm afraid an earlier attempt to get in touch with Signorina Minetti also met with a conspicuous lack of success."

"Which leaves you with me."

"One can hardly be blamed for thinking it rather more than coincidental that Mr. Paul Chavasse of the British Secret Service just happened to be on the spot when the Signorina Minetti needed some assistance."

Chavasse reached for the bottle of vodka and poured some more into his glass. "And what would you say if I told you I still didn't know what you're talking about?"

"If you persisted, you would leave me no choice. I would have to apply to the *signorina* again which would distress me greatly." Kapo sighed. "On the other hand, women are so much easier to deal with. Don't you agree, Tashko?"

The big man moved to the end of the table, a mirthless grin on his face and Chavasse nodded thoughtfully. "Somehow I thought you'd say that."

He reversed his grip on the bottle of vodka and struck sideways against Tashko's skull. The Albanian cried out sharply as the bottle smashed into pieces, drawing blood, and Chavasse heaved the table over, sending Kapo backwards in his chair, pinning him to the floor.

Haji was already moving fast across the room, a knife in his right hand. As it started to come up, Chavasse warded off the blow with one arm, caught the small man by his left wrist and, with a sudden pull, sent him crashing into the wall.

Tashko was already on his feet, blood streaming down the side of his face. He threw a tremendous punch, and Chavasse ducked under his arm and moved towards the door. Kapo pushed out a foot and tripped him so that he fell heavily to the floor.

Tashko moved in quickly, kicking at his ribs and face and Chavasse rolled away, avoiding most of the blows and scrambled up. He vaulted over the up-turned table, picked up one of the chairs in both hands and hurled it through the window with all his force. The dried and rotting wood of the frame smashed easily and the window dissolved in a snowstorm of flying glass.

He was aware of Kapo's warning cry, of Tashko lurching forward. He lashed out sideways, the edge of his hand catching the big man across the face, scrambled on to the sill and jumped into darkness.

The air rushed past his ears with a mighty roar and the fog seemed to curl around him; then he hit the water with a solid forceful smack and went down into a night that had no ending.

When he finally surfaced, he gazed up at the dark bulk of the house, at the light filtering through the fog from the smashed window. There was a sudden call, Kapo's voice drifting down, and another answered from the *Stromboli*, dimly seen in the fog to the right.

There was only one sensible way out of the situation and Chavasse took it. He turned and swam away from the landing stage, out into the harbour towards the jetty on the other side. It was perhaps a quarter of a mile, he knew that. No great distance and the water was surprisingly warm.

He took his time, swimming steadily and the voices faded into the fog behind him and he was alone in an enclosed world. Everything seemed to fade away and he felt curiously calm and at peace with himself. Time seemed to have no meaning and the riding lights of the fishing boats moored close to the jetty appeared through the fog in what seemed a remarkably short time.

He swam between them and landed at a flight of steps which led to the jetty. For a moment or two he sat there getting his breath and then went up quickly and moved along the jetty to the waterfront.

His first real need was obviously a change of clothes and he hurried through the fog towards his hotel.

After that, a visit to Orsini at the *Tabu* and perhaps a return match with Adem Kapo and his thugs although it was more than probable that the *Stromboli* was already being prepared for a hasty exit.

The electric sign over the entrance to the hotel loomed out of the night and he opened the door and moved inside. The desk was vacant, no one apparently on duty, and he went up the stairs two at a time and turned along the corridor.

The door to his room stood open, panels smashed and splintered and a light was still burning. A chair lay on its side in the middle of the floor and the blankets were scattered over the end of the bed as if there had been a struggle. He stood there for a moment, his stomach suddenly hollow, then turned and hurried back downstairs.

He noticed the foot protruding from behind the desk as he moved to the door and there was a slight, audible groan of pain. When he looked over the top, he saw the old proprietor lying on his face, blood matting the white hair at the back of the head.

6

lady in distress

The landing stage was deserted when Chavasse, Orsini and Carlo drove up in the old Ford pick-up. The big Italian cut the engine, jumped to the ground and went to the head of the steps.

He turned, shaking his head. "We're wasting our time, Paul, but we'll check the house just in case."

They went down the steps quickly and crossed the landing stage to the door. It opened without difficulty and Chavasse went up first, an old Colt automatic Orsini had given him held against his right knee.

The door to the room in which Kapo had interviewed him stood ajar, light streaming out across the dark landing. Chavasse kicked it open and waited, but there was no reply. He went in quickly at ground level, the automatic ready.

Vodka from the smashed bottle had soaked into the floor mixed with blood and the table still lay on its side. Fog billowed in through the broken window and Orsini walked across, feet crunching on glass, and peered outside.

He turned, respect on his face. "A long way down."

"I didn't have a great deal of choice. What do we do now?"

The Italian shrugged. "Go back to the *Tabu*. Maybe old Gilberto's remembered something by now."

"I wouldn't count on it," Chavasse said. "That was a hard knock he took."

"Then we'll have to think of something else."

They returned to the pick-up, crowded into the small cab and Carlo drove back to the *Tabu* through the deserted streets. As the truck braked to a halt, Chavasse checked his watch and saw that it was almost half past two. He jumped to the ground and followed the two Italians along the alley to the side door.

There were still a few customers in the bar at the front and, as they walked along the passage, the barman looked round the corner.

"Rome on the phone. They're hanging on."

"That'll be my call to s2," Chavasse said to Orsini. "I'll see what they've got to tell me about Kapo."

"I'll have another word with old Gilberto," Orsini said. "He may be thinking a little straighter by now."

Chavasse took his call in the small office at the back of the bar. The man he spoke to was the night duty officer, no one of any particular importance. Just a good reliable civil servant who knew what files were for and how to use them efficiently.

He had nothing on Kapo that Chavasse didn't

already know. Incredibly, everything the man had said about himself was true. At one time a high official in the Albanian Ministry of the Interior, he had been marked down for elimination in 1958 during one of Hoxha's earlier purges. He had been allowed to enter Italy as a political refugee and had since lived in Taranto earning a living as an import-export agent. Presumably on the basis that an Albanian of any description was preferable to a foreigner, Alb-Tourist had appointed him their Taranto agent in 1963. An official investigation by Italian Military Intelligence in that year had indicated nothing sinister in the appointment.

Chavasse thanked the duty officer. No, it was nothing of any importance. He'd simply run across Kapo during his holiday in Matano and had thought him worth checking on.

At the other end of the wire in his small office in Rome, the duty officer replaced the receiver with a thoughtful frown. Almost immediately, he picked it up again and put a call through to Bureau headquarters in London on the special line.

It could be nothing, but Chavasse was a topliner—everyone in the organization knew that. If by any remote chance he was up to anything and the Chief didn't know about it, heads might start to roll and the duty officer hadn't the slightest intention of allowing his own to be numbered among them.

The telephone on his desk buzzed sharply five minutes later and he lifted it at once. "Hello, sir . . . yes, that's right . . . well, there may be nothing in

it, but I thought you'd like to know that I've just had
a rather interesting call from Paul Chavasse in Matano . . ."

Old Gilberto coughed as the brandy caught at the
back of his throat and grinned wryly at Orsini. "I
must be getting old, Guilio. Never heard a damned
thing. It couldn't have been more than twenty minutes
after Carlo had delivered the young woman. One
moment I was reading a magazine, the next, the
lights were going out." He raised a gnarled and
scarred fist. "Old I may be, but I'd still like five
minutes on my own with that fancy bastard, whoever
he is."

Orsini grinned and patted him on the shoulder.
"You'd murder him, Gilberto. Nothing like a bit of
science to have these young toughies running round
in circles."

They went out into the passage, leaving the old
man sitting at the fire, a blanket around his shoulders.
"A good heavyweight in his day," Orsini said. "One
with the sense to get out before they scrambled his
brains. Anything from Rome?"

Chavasse shook his head. "Everything Kapo said
about himself was true. He *is* the Alb-Tourist agent
in Taranto, an old Party man from Tirana who said
the wrong thing once too often and only got out by
the skin of his teeth. According to Italian Intelligence,
he's harmless and they usually know what they're
talking about."

"That's what M.I.5 said about Fuchs and look
where it got them," Orsini pointed out. "Nobody's

perfect and the good agent is the man who manages to pull the wool over the eyes of the opposition most effectively."

"Which doesn't get us anywhere," Chavasse said. "They've gone, which is all that counts, taking Francesca Minetti with them."

They went into the office at the rear of the bar and Orsini produced a bottle of whisky and three glasses. He filled them, a slight, thoughtful frown on his face.

"Whoever took the girl, it couldn't have been Kapo and his men—the time factor wouldn't have allowed it. The men who attacked her on the jetty earlier—what can you tell me about them?"

"Judging by the language the second one used when he tried to stick his knife into me, I'd say he was Italian," Chavasse said. "Straight out of the Taranto gutter."

"Anything else interesting about him?"

"He had a dark beard, anything but the trimmed variety, and his face was badly scarred. A sort of hook shape curving into his left eye."

Orsini let out a great bellow of laughter and clapped him on the shoulder. "But my dear Paul, this is wonderful."

"You mean you know him?"

"Do I know him?" Orsini turned to Carlo. "Tell him about our good friend Toto."

"He works for a man called Vacelli," Carlo said. "A real bad one. Runs a couple of fishing boats out of here, both engaged in the Albanian trade, the town brothel and a café in the old quarter." He spat vigorously. "A pig."

"It looks as if Kapo must have employed Vacelli to get hold of the girl for him," Orsini said. "The sort of task for which Nature has fitted him admirably. Unfortunately, you arrived on the scene and messed things up."

"Which doesn't explain why Kapo went to the trouble of having me pulled in for a personal interview."

"He probably thought he could do some kind of a deal, you made a break for it and he had to leave in a hurry in case you decided to whistle down the law on him. No other choice."

"And in the meantime, Vacelli and his boys picked up the girl?"

Orsini nodded. "And Kapo had to leave before they could get in touch with him."

"So you think Vacelli may still have the girl?"

Orsini opened the drawer of his desk, took out a Luger and slipped it into his hip pocket. He smiled and the great, ugly face was quite transformed.

"Let's go and find out."

Vacelli's place fronted the harbour on the corner of an alley which led into the heart of the old town. The sign simply said *Café*. Inside, someone was playing a guitar. They parked the pick-up at the entrance and when they went in, Orsini led the way downstairs.

There was a bead curtain and the murmur of voices from the bar beyond. The guitar player sat just inside the entrance, chair balanced against the wall. He was young with dark curling hair, the sleeves of his check shirt rolled back to expose muscular arms.

Orsini pulled back the curtain and looked down at the legs sprawled across the entrance. The guitar player made no effort to move and Orsini hooked the chair from under him, the sudden clatter stunning the room to silence.

There was a narrow, marble-topped bar, the wall behind it lined with bottles and a few small tables, chairs ranged about them. The floor was of stone, the walls whitewashed and there were no more than a dozen customers, most of them men.

The guitar player came up fast, a spring knife in one hand, but Carlo was faster. His hand tightened over the wrist, twisting cruelly, and the youth screamed, dropping the knife. He staggered back against the wall, tears of pain in his eyes and Orsini shook his head.

"God knows what's happened to the youth of this country. No manners at all." He turned, looking the other patrons over casually. The bearded man with the scarred face, the one they called Toto, sat at a table by the wall, one arm in a sling.

Orsini grinned. "Eh, Toto, you don't look too good. Where's Vacelli?"

There was the scrape of a boot on stone and a surly voice growled. "What the hell do you want?"

Vacelli stood at the top of the flight of stone steps in the corner leading up to the first floor. He was built like Primo Carnera, a great ox of a man with a bullet shaped head that was too small for the rest of his body.

"Hello there, you animal," Orsini cried gaily. "We've come for the Minetti girl."

Vacelli's brutal face reddened in anger and he obviously restrained his temper with difficulty. "I don't know what you're talking about."

"What a pity." Orsini picked up the nearest chair and threw it at the shelves behind the bar, smashing the mirror and bringing down a dozen bottles. "Does that help?"

Vacelli gave a roar of rage and came down the steps on the run. Orsini picked up a full bottle of Chianti from a nearby table, jumped to one side and smashed it across Vacelli's skull as he staggered past.

Vacelli fell to one knee. Orsini picked up a chair and brought it down across the great shoulders. Vacelli grunted, started to heel over. Orsini brought the chair down again and again until it splintered into matchwood. He tossed it to one side and waited.

Slowly, painfully Vacelli reached for the edge of the bar and hauled himself up. He swayed there for a moment, then charged head-down, blood washing across his face in a red curtain. Orsini swerved and slashed him across the kidneys with the edge of his hand as Vacelli plunged past him.

Vacelli screamed and fell on his face. He tried to push himself up, slobbering like an animal, but it was no good. He collapsed with a great sigh and lay still.

"Anyone else?" Orsini demanded.

No one moved and he turned to Carlo. "Watch things down here. We won't be long."

Chavasse followed him up the stairs and the big

Italian pulled back a curtain and led the way along a narrow passage. A young woman in a cheap nylon housecoat leaned in a doorway smoking a cigarette.

"Eh, Guilio, have you killed the bastard?"

"Just about." He grinned. "He'll be inactive for quite a while. Time enough for you to pack your bags and move on. There was a girl brought here tonight. Any idea where she is?"

"The end room. He was just going in when you arrived. I don't think he meant her any good."

"My thanks, *carissima*." Orsini kissed her lightly on one cheek. "Go home to your mother."

Chavasse was already ahead of him, but the door was locked. "Francesca, it's Paul," he called.

There was a quick movement inside and she called back, "The door's locked on the outside."

Orsini stood back, raised one booted foot and stamped twice against the lock. There was a sudden splintering sound, the door sagged on its hinges, rotten wood crumbling. He stamped again and it fell back against the wall.

Francesca Minetti stood waiting, her face very white. She was still wearing Chavasse's old sweater and looked about fifteen years old. Chavasse was aware of the breath hissing sharply between Orsini's teeth and then the Italian was moving forward quickly.

His voice was strangely gentle and comforting, like a father reassuring a frightened child. "It's all right now, *cara*. There is nothing to worry about any more."

She held his hand, gazing up into the ugly, battered

face and tried to smile and then she started to tremble. She turned, stumbled across the wreckage of the door and ran into Chavasse's arms.

7

passage by night

It was just after eight o'clock on the following evening when the *Buona Esperanza* moved away from the jetty and turned out to sea. It was a warm, soft night with a luminosity shining from the water. There was no moon, for heavy cloud banked over the horizon as though a storm might be in the offing.

Orsini was at the wheel and Chavasse stood beside him, leaning forward to peer through the curved deckhouse window into the darkness ahead.

"What about the weather?" he said.

"Force four wind with rain imminent. Nothing to worry about."

"Is it the same for the Drin Gulf?"

"A few fog patches, but they'll be more of a help than anything else."

Chavasse lit two cigarettes and handed one to the Italian. "Funny what a day-to-day business life is.

I never expected to set foot on Albanian soil again."

"The things we do for the ladies," Orsini grinned. "But this one is something special, Paul. This I assure you as an expert. She reminds me very much of my wife, God rest her."

Chavasse looked at him curiously. "I never knew you'd been married."

"A long time ago." Orsini's face was calm, untroubled, but the sadness was there in his voice. "She was only nineteen when we married. That was in 1941 during my naval service. We spent one leave together, that's all. The following year she was killed in an air raid while staying with her mother in Milan."

There was nothing to be said and Chavasse stood there in silence. After a while, Orsini increased speed. "Take over, Paul. I'll plot our course."

Chavasse slipped behind him and the Italian moved to the chart table. For some time he busied himself with the charts and finally nodded in satisfaction.

"We should move into the marshes just before dawn." He placed a cheroot between his teeth and grinned. "What happens after that is in the lap of God."

"Do you want me to spell you for a while?" Chavasse asked.

Orsini took over the wheel again and shook his head. "Later, Paul, after Carlo has done his trick. That way I'll be fresh for the run-in at dawn."

Chavasse left him there and went down to the galley where he discovered Francesca making coffee. He leaned in the doorway and grinned. "That's what I like about Italian girls. So good in the kitchen."

She turned and smiled mischievously. "Is that all we're good for—cooking?"

She wore a pair of old denim pants and a heavy sweater and the long hair was plaited into a single pigtail which hung across one shoulder. She looked incredibly fresh and alive and Chavasse shook his head.

"I could think of one or two things, but the timing's wrong."

"What about the terrace of the British Embassy?"

"Too public."

She poured coffee into a mug and handed it to him. "There's a place I know in the hills outside Rome. Only a village inn, but the food is out of this world. You eat it by candlelight on a terrace overlooking a hillside covered with vines. The fireflies dance in the wind and you can smell the flowers for a week afterwards. It's an experience one shouldn't miss."

"I'm all tied up for the next couple of days," Chavasse said, "but after that, I'm free most evenings."

"By a strange coincidence, so am I. I'm also in the telephone book and I'd like to point out that you still owe me a date."

"Now how could I forget a thing like that?"

He ducked as she threw a crust of dry bread at his head, turned and went through the aft cabin into the saloon. Carlo had two aqualungs and their ancillary equipment laid out on the table.

"There's fresh coffee in the galley," Chavasse told him.

"I'll get some later. I want to finish checking this lot."

He never had much to say for himself, a strange, silent youth, but a good man to have at your back in trouble and devoted to Orsini. He sat on the edge of the table, a cigarette smouldering between his lips and worked his way methodically through the various items of equipment. Chavasse watched him for a while, then went through into the other cabin.

He lay staring at the bulkhead, thinking about the task ahead. If Francesca's memory hadn't failed her and the cross-bearing she had given them was accurate, then the whole thing was simple. There couldn't be more than five or six fathoms of water in those lagoons and the recovery of the statue shouldn't take long. With any kind of luck, they could be back in Matano within twenty-four hours.

He could hear a rumble of voices from the galley, Francesca quite distinctly, and then Carlo laughed, which was something unusual. Chavasse was conscious of a slight, unreasoning pang of jealousy. He lay there thinking about her and the voices merged with the throbbing of the engine and the rattle of water against the hull.

He was not conscious of having slept, only of being awake and checking his watch and realizing with a shock that it was two a.m. Orsini was sleeping on the far bunk, his face calm, one arm behind his head and Chavasse pulled on his reefer coat and went on deck.

Mist swirled from the water and the *Buona Esperanza* kicked along at a tremendous pace. There was no moon, but stars were scattered across the sky like diamonds in a black velvet cushion and there was still that strange luminosity in the water.

Carlo was standing at the wheel, his head disembodied in the light from the binnacle. Chavasse moved in and lit a cigarette. "How are we doing?"

"Fine," Carlo said. "Keep her on one-four-oh till three a.m. then alter course to one-four-five. Guilio said he'd be up around four. We should be near the coast by then."

The door banged behind him and a small trapped wind lifted the charts, raced round the deckhouse looking for a way out and died in a corner. Chavasse pulled a seat down from the wall and sat back, his hands steady on the wheel.

This was what he liked more than anything else. To be alone with the sea and the night and a boat. Something deep in his subconscious, some race image handed on from his Breton ancestors, responded to the challenge. Men who had loved the sea more than any woman, who had sailed to the Grand Banks of the North American coast to fish for cod, long before Columbus or the Cabots had dreamed of crossing the Atlantic.

The door opened suddenly as rain dashed against the window and he was aware of the heavy aroma of coffee, together with another, more subtle fragrance.

"What's wrong with bed at this time in the morning?" he demanded.

She chuckled softly. "Oh, this is much more fun. How are we doing?"

"Dead on course. Another hour and Orsini takes over for the final run-in."

She pulled a seat down beside him, balanced her

tray on the chart table and poured coffee into two mugs. "What about a sandwich?"

He was surprised at the keenness of his appetite and they ate in a companionable and intimate silence, thighs touching. Afterwards, he gave her a cigarette and she poured more coffee.

"What do you think our chances are, Paul?" she said. "The truth now."

"All depends on how accurately your brother plotted the final position of the launch when she sank. If we can find her without too much trouble, the rest should be plain sailing. Diving for the Madonna will be no great trick in water of that depth. Depending on weather conditions, we could be on our way back by this evening."

"And you don't anticipate any trouble in the Drin Gulf?"

"From the Albanian Navy?" he shook his head. "From an efficiency point of view, it's almost non-existent. The Russians had a lot of stuff based here before the big bust-up, but they withdrew when Hoxha refused to toe the line. Something he hadn't reckoned on and China's too far away to give him that kind of assistance."

"What a country." She shook her head. "I can well believe the old story about God having nothing but trouble left to give when it came to Albania's turn."

Chavasse nodded. "Not exactly a happy history."

"A succession of conquerors, more than any other country in Europe. Greeks, Romans, Goths, Byzantines, Serbs, Bulgars, Sicilians, Venetians, Normans and Turks. They've all held the country for varying periods."

"And always, the people have struggled to be free." Chavasse shook his head. "How ironic life can be. After centuries of desperately fighting for independence, Albania receives it, only to find herself in the grip of a tyranny worse than any that has gone before."

"Is it really as bad as they say?"

He nodded. "The *sigurmi* are everywhere. Even the Italian Workers' Holiday Association complain that they get one *sigurmi* agent allocated to each member of their holiday parties. Even at a rough estimate, Hoxha and his boys have purged better than one hundred thousand people since he took over and you know yourself how the various religious groups have been treated. Stalin would have been proud of him. An apt pupil."

She obviously found the subject distressing and he remembered the members of her family who had suffered and could have kicked himself for having gone into such detail.

He took out his cigarettes quickly and offered her one. She smoked silently for a while and then said slowly, "Last year, two of your people who were operating temporarily through s2 in Rome went missing. One in Albania, the other in Turkey."

Chavasse nodded. "Matt Sorley and Jules Dumont. Good men both."

"How can you go on living the life you do? That sort of thing must happen a lot. Look how close you came to not getting out of Tirana."

"Maybe I just never grew up," he said lightly. "The perennial schoolboy playing cops and robbers or Robin Hood in the playground."

"How did it all begin?"

"Quite by chance. I was lecturing in languages at a British university, a friend wanted to pull a relative out of Czechoslovakia and I gave him a hand. That's when the Chief pulled me in. At that time he was interested in people who spoke Eastern European languages."

"An unusual accomplishment."

"Some people can work out cube roots in their heads in seconds, others never forget anything they ever read. I have the same sort of kink for languages. I soak them up like a sponge—no effort."

She lapsed into fluent Albanian. "Isn't it a little unnerving? Don't you ever get your wires crossed?"

"Not that I can recall," he replied faultlessly in the same language. "I can't afford that kind of mistake. If it's any consolation, I still can't read a Chinese newspaper. On the other hand, I've only ever met two Europeans who could."

"With that kind of flair plus your academic training you could pick up a chair in modern languages at almost any university in Britain or the States," she said. "Doesn't the thought appeal to you?"

"Not in the slightest. I got into this sort of work by chance and by chance, I possessed all the virtues needed to make me good at it."

"You mean you actually enjoy it?"

"Something like that. If I'd been born in Germany twenty years earlier, I'd probably have ended up in the Gestapo. If I'd been born an Albanian, I might well have been a most efficient member of the *sigurmi*. Who knows?"

She seemed shocked. "I don't believe you."

"Why not? It takes a certain type of man—or woman—to do our kind of work—a professional. I can recognize the quality, and appreciate it, in my opposite numbers. I don't see anything wrong in that."

There was a strained silence and he knew that in some way he had disappointed her. She reached for the tray. "I'd better take these below. We must be getting close."

The door closed behind her and Chavasse opened the window and breathed in the sharp morning air feeling rather sad. So often people like her, the fringe crowd who did the paper work, manned the radios, decoded the messages, could never really know what it was like in the field. What it took to survive. Well, he, Paul Chavasse, had survived and not by waving any flags, either.

Then what in the hell are you doing here? he asked himself and a rueful smile crossed his face. What was it Orsini had said? *The things we do for the ladies.* And he was right, this one *was* something special— something very special.

The door swung open and Orsini entered, immense in his old reefer coat, and peaked cap on the side of his head. "Everything all right, Paul?"

Chavasse nodded and handed over the wheel. "Couldn't be better."

Orsini lit another of his inevitable cheroots. "Good. Shouldn't be long now."

Dawn seeped into the sky, a grey, half-light with a heavy mist rolling across the water. Orsini asked Chavasse to take over again and consulted the charts. He checked the cross-bearing Francesca had given him and traced a possible course in from the sea through the maze of channels marked on the chart.

"Everything okay?" Chavasse asked.

Orsini came back to the wheel and shrugged. "I know these charts. Four or five fathoms and strong tidal current. That means that one day there's a sandbank, the next, ten fathoms of clear water. Estuary marshes are always the same. We'll go in through the main outlet of the Buene and turn into the marshes about half a mile inland. Not only safer, but a damned sight quicker."

The mist enfolded them until they were running through a strange enclosed world. Orsini reduced speed to ten knots and, a few moments later, Carlo and Francesca came up from below.

Chavasse went and stood in the prow, hands in pockets and the marshes drifted out of the mist and their stench filled the nostrils. Wildfowl called overhead on their way in from the sea and Carlo moved beside him and crossed himself.

"A bad place, this. Always, I am glad to leave."

It was a landscape from a nightmare. Long, narrow sandbanks lifted from the water and inland, mile upon mile of marsh grass and great reeds marched into the mist, interlaced by a thousand creeks and lagoons.

Orsini reduced speed to three knots and leaned

from the side window, watching the reeds drift by on either hand. Chavasse moved along the deck and looked up at him.

"How far are we from the position Francesca gave?"

"Perhaps three miles, but the going would be too difficult. In a little while we must carry on in the dinghy. Much safer."

"And who minds the launch?"

"Carlo—it's all arranged. He isn't pleased, but then he seldom is about anything."

He grinned down at Carlo who glared up at him and went below. Chavasse moved back along the deck and joined Francesca in the prow. A few moments later the launch entered a small lagoon, perhaps a hundred feet in diameter and Orsini cut the engines.

They glided forward and grounded gently against a sandbank as he came out on deck and joined them. He slipped an arm around Francesca's shoulders and smiled down at her.

"Not long now, *cara*. A few more hours and we'll be on our way home again. I, Guilio Orsini, promise you."

She looked up at him gravely, then turned to Chavasse, a strange, shadowed expression in her eyes and for some unaccountable reason, he shivered.

8

full fathom five

Francesca cooked a hot meal, perhaps the last they would have for some time, and afterwards Carlo and Chavasse broke out the large rubber dinghy, inflated it and attached the outboard motor.

When they went below for the aqualung, Orsini was sitting on the edge of the table loading a machine pistol. The top of one of the saloon seats had been removed and inside there was a varied assortment of weapons. The sub machine gun, a couple of automatic rifles and an old Bren of the type used by the British infantry during the war.

"Help yourself," he said. "A selection to suit all tastes."

Chavasse picked up one of the automatic rifles, a Garrand, and nodded. "This will do me. What about ammo?"

"There should be plenty in there somewhere."

There were three boxes stacked together. The first contained grenades, the second, several pouched bandoliers. Chavasse picked one up and Orsini shook his head.

"That's an explosive we used during the war for underwater sabotage. I've had it for years."

"A hell of a thing to have people sitting on," Chavasse said.

Orsini grinned. "Just the thing for fishing. You stick a chemical detonator in a piece as big as your fist, heave it over the side and wait. They come floating up by the thousand. I'll take some along, just in case we need to do any blasting."

Chavasse found the ammunition in another box, loaded his Garrand and strapped a bandolier containing a hundred rounds about his waist. He helped Carlo up top with one of the aqualungs and they stowed it in the prow of the dinghy along with several other items of equipment. As they finished, Orsini and Francesca came up on deck.

She was wearing an old reefer coat of Carlo's against the cold, the sleeves rolled back and a scarf was tied around her head, peasant-fashion. She seemed calm, but was extremely pale and there were blue shadows under her eyes.

Chavasse squeezed her hand as he helped her into the dinghy and whispered, "Soon be over. We'll be on our way out again before you know it."

She smiled wanly, but made no reply, and he clambered into the dinghy beside her and sat on one side, the Garrand across his knees. Orsini followed, seating himself in the stern. He glanced up at Carlo and grinned.

"If all goes well, we could be back by this evening. Certainly no later than dawn tomorrow."

"And if it doesn't?"

"Always you look on the dark side."

Orsini pressed the automatic starter and the powerful motor roared into life. Wildfowl rose from the reeds in alarm, the sound of them filling the air. As Carlo released the line, the dinghy moved forward quickly. Chavasse had one final glimpse of his dark, saturnine face scowling at them over the rail and then the marsh moved in to enfold them.

The reeds lifted out of the mist like pale ghosts on either hand and the only sound was the steady rattle of the outboard motor. Orsini consulted his compass, turning from one narrow waterway to the other, moving always towards the position on the chart which Francesca had given them.

She sat in silence, her hands buried in the pockets of the reefer coat and Chavasse watched, wondering what she was thinking. About her brother, probably. Of his death and her own struggle for survival in this waking nightmare. The stench of the marshes, heavy and penetrating, filled his nostrils and he hurriedly lit a cigarette.

It was perhaps an hour later that they emerged into a broad waterway and Orsini cut the motor. "This is as near as I can make it from the position you gave me," he told Francesca. "Recognize anything?"

She stood up and gazed around her. When she sat down, there was a troubled look on her face. "They all look the same, these waterways, but I'm sure this wasn't the place. It was much smaller. I can remember my brother running the boat into the reeds to hide her and then we suddenly emerged into this small lagoon."

Orsini stood up and looked around, but the reeds stretched into the mist, an apparently impenetrable barrier. He turned to Chavasse and shrugged. "This is definitely the position he charted so this lagoon she speaks of can't be far away. We'll have to go looking for it, that's all."

Chavasse started to undress. "I hope to God those last malaria shots I had are still active."

He kept on his shirt, pants and shoes against the cold, went over the side and struck across the channel. Orsini followed a moment or so later and swam into the mist in the opposite direction.

It was bitterly cold and Chavasse coughed, retching as the strong earthy stench caught at the back of his throat. He swam into the reeds, following a narrow waterway that turned in a circle bringing him back into the main channel.

He tried another, emerging a few moments later into a shallow lagoon no more than four or five feet deep and he swam across into the reeds, forcing his way through. Just then, Orsini called through the mist from the other side of the barrier and Chavasse pushed towards him. He came out on the perimeter of a small lagoon no more than a hundred feet across, as Orsini surfaced in the centre.

The Italian floated there, coughing a little, hair plastered across his forehead. Chavasse looked down at the launch mirrored in five fathoms of clear water, then did a steep surface dive.

He swallowed to ease the pressure in his ears, then grabbed for the deck rail and hung there. The launch had tilted over on the shelving bottom and he worked his way round to the stern were he found the name *Teresa—Bari* inscribed in gold paint across the counter. He had a quick look at the general condition of the wreck, then released his hold and shot to the surface.

He trod water, gasping for air and grinned at Orsini. "Good navigating."

"My mother, God rest her, always told me I was a genius."

Orsini turned and swam across the lagoon, plunging into the reeds and Chavasse followed. They emerged into the main channel within sight of the dinghy and swam towards it.

"Any luck?" Francesca asked.

Orsini nodded. "Just as you described. So near and yet so far. Without that cross-bearing it would have been hopeless. One could have searched these marshes for a year without finding anything."

They climbed back into the dinghy and he started the motor and steered for the wall of reeds. For a moment, they seemed an impossible barrier and Chavasse and Francesca pulled desperately with all their strength. Quite suddenly, the reeds parted and the dinghy passed into the lagoon.

Orsini cut the motor and they drifted towards the

centre. Francesca gazed over the side, down through the clear water, her face very pale. She shivered abruptly and looked up.

"Will it take long?"

Orsini shook his head. "We'll fix a line to hold us in position and one of us will go down using the aqualung. With luck we'll be out of here in a couple of hours." He turned to Chavasse. "Feel like another swim?"

Chavasse nodded. "Why not? It couldn't be any colder than it is up here."

The wind sliced through his wet shirt like a bayonet as he lifted the heavy aqualung on his back and Orsini strapped it into place. Francesca watched, eyes very large in the white face and Chavasse grinned.

"A piece of cake. We'll be out of here before you know it."

She forced a smile and he pulled on his diving mask, sat on the rail and allowed himself to fall back into the water. As he surfaced, Orsini tossed him a line. Chavasse went under, paused to adjust his air supply and swam down towards the launch in a sweeping curve.

The *Teresa* was almost bottom up and he hovered over the stern rail to attach the end of his line and then swam towards the deckhouse which was jammed against the sandy bottom of the lagoon at a steep angle.

There were jagged bullet holes in the hull and superstructure, mute evidence of the fight between the *Teresa* and the Albanian patrol boat. Some sort of a direct hit had been scored on the roof of the saloon and the companionway was badly damaged, the only entrance being a narrow aperture.

He managed it, pulling himself through by force, the aqualung scraping protestingly against the jagged edges of the metal. The saloon table had broken free of its floor fastenings and floated against the bulkhead together with several bottles and the leather cushions from the saloon.

There was no sign of the Madonna or anything remotely resembling it and he swam towards the door leading to the forward cabin. The roof at this point had been smashed in by what looked like a cannon shell and a twisted mass of metal blocked the door. He turned and swam out through the saloon, squeezed through the entrance and struck up towards the light.

He surfaced a few feet astern of the dinghy and swam towards it. Orsini gave him a hand over the side and Chavasse crouched in the bottom and pushed up his mask.

"The interior's in one hell of a mess. Stuff all over the place."

"And the Madonna?"

"No sign at all. I couldn't get into the inner cabin. There's a lot of wreckage at that end of the saloon and the door's jammed."

"But that is where it is!" Francesca said. "I remember now. Marco put it under one of the bunks for greater safety when the shooting started. It was wrapped in a blanket and bound in oilskin against the damp. The whole bundle was about five feet long."

Orsini pulled a package from under the stern seat.

"A good thing I brought along some of that explosive. You'll have to blast your way in."

He unfolded a bandolier and took out a piece of the plastic explosive shaped like a sausage. "That should be enough. We don't want to blow the whole boat apart."

From another bundle he took a small wooden box containing several chemical pencil detonators, each one carefully packed in a plastic sheath.

"How long do these things give me?" Chavasse demanded.

"A full minute. I've got some which take longer, but I left them on the boat."

"Well, thanks very much, friend," Chavasse said. "What are you hoping to do—collect on my insurance?"

"A minute should be plenty. All you have to do is insert the fuse, break the end and get out of it. I'll go myself if you like."

"Stop trying to show off," Chavasse jeered. "In any case, you'd never get that frame of yours in through the saloon companionway."

He was conscious of Francesca's face, white and troubled as he gripped the rubber mouthpiece of his breathing tube between his teeth, pulled down his mask and went backwards over the side.

He went down through the clear water quickly, negotiated the companionway with no trouble and moved inside. He jammed the plastic explosive into the corner at the bottom of the door, inserted the detonator carefully. For a moment, he floated there looking at it, then he snapped the end.

The fuse started to burn at once, fizzing like a firecracker and he turned and swam for the companionway. As he squeezed through the narrow opening, his aqualung snagged on the jagged metal. He paused, fighting back the panic and eased himself through. A moment later he was free and shooting towards the surface.

He broke through at the side of the dinghy and Orsini pulled him over. Almost immediately, there was a muffled roar and the dinghy rocked in the turbulence. The surface of the water boiled and wreckage bobbed up, sand and mud spreading in a great stain towards the reeds.

They waited for fifteen minutes, and gradually, the water cleared again and the hull of the launch became visible. Orsini nodded and Chavasse went over the side.

There was still a lot of sand and mud hanging in suspension like a great curtain, obscuring his vision, but not seriously, and he went down towards *Teresa*.

The explosion had even disturbed the entrance to the companionway, the turbulence blowing the wreckage back out on to the deck and he passed through the saloon himself with no trouble.

Where the door to the cabin had been, there was now only a gaping hole and he swam forward, paused for a moment and then moved inside.

The tiered bunks were still intact, but bedding floated against the bulkhead, moving languorously in the water like some living thing. He pushed his way through their pale fronds and looked for the Madonna. It became immediately obvious that he was wasting his time. There was no five foot bundle wrapped in oilskins as Francesca had described.

The Madonna was carved out of ebony, a heavy wood, but one that would float, and he drifted up through the waving blankets, pulling them to one side, searching desperately, but he was wasting his time.

Back outside, he grabbed for the stern rail and floated there like some strange sea creature, his webbed feet hanging down. Perhaps Francesca had been wrong. Maybe her brother had moved it to some other place in the launch. And there was always the chance that it had been blown clear in the explosion.

He decided to start again, working his way from one end of the launch to the other. But first he had to let Orsini know what had happened.

He surfaced a few feet away from the dinghy and went under again in the same moment. Orsini was standing with his back to him, hands above his head. On the far side of the dinghy was a flat bottomed marsh punt, an outboard motor at its stern. Its occupants were three Albanians in drab and dirty uniforms, in their peaked caps the red star of the Army of the Republic. Two of them menaced Orsini and Francesca with sub machine guns while the third was in the act of stepping across.

Chavasse went under the dinghy in a shallow dive as sub machine gun fire churned the water where he had surfaced. His aqualung scraped the bottom of the punt and he reached up, grabbed the thwart and pulled the frail craft completely over.

One of the soldiers sprawled against him, legs thrashing in a panic and Chavasse slipped an arm around his neck and took him into deep water. His legs scraped painfully against the stern rail of *Teresa* and he hung on with one hand, tightening his grip.

The soldier's face twisted to one side, hands clawing back, wrenching the breathing tube from his assailant's mouth. Chavasse tightened his lips and hung on. The man's limbs moved in slow motion, weakening perceptibly until suddenly, he stopped struggling altogether. Chavasse released his grip and the body spun away from him.

The sand at the bottom of the lagoon had churned into a great cloud and he clamped the mouthpiece of his breathing tube between his teeth and struck out for the surface. Above him, there was a tremendous disturbance, limbs thrashing together in a violent struggle.

He came up into the centre of it, pulling his knife from his sheath, and struck out at a dim, khaki-clad shape. The soldier bucked agonizingly, shoving Chavasse away so that he broke through to the surface.

A couple of yards away from him, a fifteen foot motor boat bumped against the dinghy. He was aware of Francesca struggling in the grip of two soldiers, of Orsini floating against the hull, blood on his face.

A soldier rushed to the rail, machine gun levelled, and a man in a dark leather coat with a high fur collar ran forward and knocked the barrel to one side, the bullets discharging themselves harmlessly in the sky.

"Alive! I want him alive!"

For one brief moment Chavasse looked up into Adem Kapo's excited face, then he jack-knifed and went down through the water, his webbed feet driving him towards the edge of the lagoon. He swam into the reeds, forcing his way through desperately. A few moments later he surfaced. Behind him, he could hear voices calling excitedly and then the engine of the motor boat coughed into life.

He broke through into the main channel, moved straight across it into a narrow tributary and started to swim for his life.

9

enter liri kupi

The motor boat turned out of a side channel into the main stream of the Buene River, the dinghy trailing behind on a line. In the stern, four soldiers huddled together, smoking cigarettes and talking in low tones. The bodies of their two comrades, killed in the lagoon by Chavasse, lay under a tarpaulin beside them.

Orsini was handcuffed to the rail and seemed half unconscious, his head roughly bandaged where a rifle butt had struck him a glancing blow. There was no sign of Francesca Minetti, but Adem Kapo paced the foredeck, impatiently smoking a cigarette, the fur collar of his hunting jacket turned up.

Orsini watched him, eyes half-closed, and after a while, another man appeared from the companionway. He was as big as Orsini with a scarred, brutal face and wore the uniform of a colonel in the Army of the Albanian Republic with the green insignia of the

Intelligence corps on his collar.

Kapo turned on him, eyes like black holes in the white face. "Well?"

The colonel shrugged. "She isn't being very helpful."

The anger blazed out of the little man like a searing flame. "You said it would work, damn you. That all we had to do was wait and they'd walk right into the net. What in the hell am I supposed to tell them in Tirana?"

"What do you think he's going to do, swim out of here?" The big man laughed coldly. "We'll run him down, never fear. A night out on his own in a place like this will shrink him down to size."

"Let's hope you're right."

Kapo walked across to Orsini, looked down at him for a moment, then kicked him savagely in the side. Orsini stifled the cry of pain which rose in his throat and continued to feign unconsciousness. Kapo turned away and resumed his pacing.

As the motor boat rounded a point of land jutting from the mist into the river, Chavasse parted the reeds carefully. He stood up to his chest in water no more than fifteen yards away as it passed and his trained eyes took in everything—Orsini and the soldiers, Kapo standing in the prow, the cigarette holder jutting from a corner of his mouth.

The most interesting thing was the presence of Taskho. When Chavasse had last encountered him, he had been dressed like any seaman off the Taranto waterfront; now he wore the uniform of a colonel in the Albanian Intelligence Corps, which explained a lot. Beyond him, through the deckhouse window, Chavasse could just see the head and shoulders of Haji, the knife man, standing at the wheel.

The motor boat passed into the mist and he waded on to a piece of comparatively dry land to take stock of the situation. The stench of the marsh filled his nostrils and the bitter cold ate into his bones, numbing his brain, making it difficult to think straight.

There was a hell of a lot about the whole affair that didn't make any kind of sense, but the basic situation was obvious enough. Adem Kapo was no ordinary agent, but someone a whole lot more important than that. Probably a high ranking *sigurmi* officer. He'd have to be to have a Colonel of Intelligence taking orders from him.

In any event he was a man who knew what he was doing. He'd obviously sailed straight for the Buene from Matano and his twenty-four hour start had given him the time he'd needed to reach Tama and organize a suitable reception.

The *Buona Esperanza* must have been under observation from the moment it hit the coast and tracking the dinghy would have been no great trick to men who knew the marshes.

He wondered what had happened to Carlo? He too was probably on his way to Tama by now. It was the only sizeable town in the area and certain to be Kapo's base.

The engine of the motor boat faded into the distance and he slid into the water and started to swim after it. Within an hour at the outside, they'd be out in force looking for him, probably concentrating their search towards the coast.

Under the circumstances, Tama would probably be a whole lot safer. At least there would be houses scattered along the river bank, and where there were houses there was dry clothes and food. There might even be a chance of doing something about the others, although he didn't hold out much hope of that.

About fifteen minutes later the air in his aqualung ran out. He surfaced quickly and waded from the river into the reeds. He pulled off his rubber flippers, unbuckled the heavy aqualung and let it sink into the ooze.

He went forward through the reeds and the wild-fowl called as they lifted from the water, disturbed by his passing. After a while he came out on higher ground and moved on through the mist, keeping the river on his left.

It was hard going through mud flats and marsh, and constantly he had to wade across narrow creeks, often sinking up to his waist in thick, glutinous mud. The salt water stung his eyes painfully and the intense cold steadily drove every trace of warmth from his body until his limbs had lost all feeling.

He moved into the grey curtain and the ground became firmer and he found himself stumbling across firm sand and springy marsh grass. He paused on a small hillock, head turned slightly to one side. He could smell woodsmoke, heavy and pungent on the air, drifting before the wind.

A narrow arm of the river encircled a small island and a low house looked from the mist. There was no sign of life and no boat was moored at the narrow wooden jetty. Probably the home of a fisherman or wildfowler out at his traps. Chavasse moved upstream, disturbing a wild duck, and walked into the river, allowing the current to sweep him in towards the island.

He landed in the reeds and moved through them carefully, drawing his knife. The house was no more than twenty yards away, a poor enough looking place of rough hewn logs with a shingle roof and stone chimney.

Two or three scrawny hens picked apathetically at the soil and scattered as he moved across the patch of open ground. The back door was simply several heavy wooden planks nailed together and it opened with a protesting groan as he unfastened the chain which held it.

He moved into a small dark room that was obviously some sort of kitchen. There was a cupboard, a rough table and a pail of fresh water at the side of the door. The living room was furnished with a table and several chairs. There were two or three cupboards and a skin rug covered the wooden floor in front of the stone hearth on which logs burned fitfully, heavily banked by ashes.

He crouched to the warmth, spreading his hands and a cold wind seemed to touch the side of his face. A voice said quietly, "Easy now. Hands behind your neck and don't try anything stupid."

He came up slowly. There was a soft footstep and the hard barrel of a gun was pushed against his back. As a hand reached for the hilt of the knife at his waist, he pivoted to the left, swinging away from the gun barrel. There was a cry of dismay as they came together and fell heavily to the floor. Chavasse raised his right arm to bring down the edge of his hand in the deadly *karate* blow that is as lethal as a woodsman's axe.

He paused. His opponent was a young girl, perhaps nineteen or twenty, certainly no more. She wore a heavy waterproof hunting jacket, corduroy breeches and leather knee boots and her dark hair was close-cropped like a young boy's, the skin sallow over high cheekbones, the eyes dark brown. She was not beautiful and yet in any crowd she would have stood out.

"Now there's a thing," he said softly and sat back.

For a moment, she lay there, eyes widening in surprise and then, in a flash, she was on her feet again like a cat, the hunting rifle in her hands.

She stood there, feet apart, the barrel steady on his chest and he waited. The barrel wavered, sank slowly. She leaned the rifle against the table and examined him curiously. Her eyes took in his bare feet, the shirt and pants that were clinging to his body.

She nodded. "You're on the run, aren't you? Where from? The chain gang at Tama?"

He shook his head. "I'm on the run all right, angel, but not from there."

She scowled and reached for the rifle again. "You're no *gegh*, that's for sure. You speak like a *tosk* from the big city."

Chavasse was well aware of the enmity which still existed between the two main racial groups in Albania. The *geghs* of the north with their loyalty to family and tribe and the *tosks* of the south from whom Communism had sprung.

There were times when a man had to play a hunch and this was one of them. His face split into that inimitable charming smile that was one of his greatest assets and he raised a hand as the rifle was turned again.

"Neither *gegh* nor *tosk*. I'm an outlander."

Her face was a study of bewilderment. "An outlander? From where? Yugoslavia?"

He shook his head. "Italy."

Understanding dawned. "Ah, a smuggler."

"Something like that. We were surprised by the military. I managed to get away. I think they've taken my friends to Tama." She stood watching him, a thoughtful frown on her face and he made the final gesture and held out his hand. "Paul Chavasse."

"French?" she said.

"And English. A little of both."

She made her decision and her hand reached for his. "Liri Kupi."

"There was a *gegh* chieftain called Abas Kupi, leader of the *Legliteti*, the royalist party."

"Head of our clan. He fled to Italy after the Communists murdered most of his friends at a so-called friendship meeting."

"You don't sound as if you care for Hoxha and his friends very much?"

"Hoxha?"

She spat vigorously and accurately into the fire.

10

the jaws of the tiger

Chavasse stood on a rush mat beside the large bed and rubbed himself down with a towel until his flesh glowed. He dressed quickly in the clothes Liri had provided; corduroy pants, a checked wool shirt and kneelength leather boots a size too large so that he took them off again and pulled on an extra pair of socks.

The clothes had belonged to her brother. Conscripted into the army at eighteen, he had been killed in one of the many patrol clashes which took place almost daily along the Yugoslavian border. Her father had died fighting with the *Legliteti*, the royalist party, in the mountains in the last year of the war. Since the death of her mother she had lived alone in the marshes where she had been born and bred, earning her living from wildfowling.

She was crouched at the fire when he went back

into the living room, stirring something in a large pot suspended from a hook. She turned and smiled, pushing back the hair from her forehead.

"All you need now is some food inside you."

He pulled a chair to the table, his stomach contracting as she spooned a hot stew on to a tin plate. He wasted no time on conversation, but picked up his spoon and started to eat. When the plate was empty, she filled it again.

He sat back with a sigh. "They couldn't have done better at the London Hilton."

She opened a bottle and filled a glass with a colourless liquid. "I'd like to offer you some coffee, but it's very hard to come by these days. This is a spirit we distil ourselves. Very potent if you're not used to it, but it can be guaranteed to keep out the marsh fever."

It exploded in Chavasse's stomach and spread through his body in a warm glow. He coughed several times and tears sprang to his eyes.

"Now this, they wouldn't be able to offer, even at the London Hilton."

She opened an old tin carefully and offered him a cigarette. They were Macedonian, coarse, brown tobacco loose in the paper, but Chavasse knew how to handle them. He screwed the end round expertly and leaned across the table as she held out a burning splinter from the fire.

She lit a cigarette herself, blew out a cloud of pungent smoke and said calmly, "You're no smuggler, I can see that. No seaman, either. Your hands are too nice."

"So I lied."

"You must have had a good reason."

He frowned down into his glass for a moment, then decided to go ahead. "You've heard of the Virgin of Scutari?"

"The Black Madonna? Who hasn't? Her statue disappeared about three months ago. The general opinion is that the central government in Tirana had it stolen. They're worried because people have been turning to the church again lately."

"I came to the Buene looking for it," Chavasse said. "It was supposed to be on board a launch which sank in one of the lagoons in the marsh towards the coast. My friends and I were searching for it when the military turned up."

He told her about Francesca Minetti or as much as she needed to know and of Guilio Orsini and Carlo and the *Buona Esperanza*. When he was done, she nodded slowly.

"A bad business. The *sigurmi* will squeeze them dry, even this smuggler friend of yours. They have their ways and they are not pleasant. I'm sorry for the girl. God knows what they will do with her."

"I was wondering whether it would be possible to get into Tama," Chavasse said. "Perhaps find out what's happened to them?"

She looked at him sharply, her face grave. "We have a saying. Only a fool puts his head between the jaws of the Tiger."

"They'll be beating the marshes towards the coast," he said. "That stands to reason. Who's going to look for me in Tama?"

"A good point." She got to her feet and looked down into the fire, her hand on the stone mantel above it. She turned to face him. "There is one person who might be able to help, a Franciscan, Father Shedu. In the war, he was a famous resistance fighter in the hills, a legend in his own time. It would hardly be polite to arrest or shoot such a man. They content themselves with making life difficult for him—always with the utmost politeness, of course. He hasn't been here long. A couple of months or so. I think the last man was taken away."

"I could make a good guess about what happened to him," Chavasse said. "This Father Shedu, he's in Tama now?"

"There's a mediaeval monastery on the outskirts of the town. They use it as local military headquarters. The Catholic church has been turned into a restaurant, but there's an old monastery chapel at the water's edge. Father Shedu holds his services there."

"Would it be difficult to reach?"

"From here?" she shrugged. "Not more than half an hour. I have an outboard motor. Not too reliable, but it gets me there."

"Could I borrow it?"

"Oh, no." She shook her head. "They'd pick you up before you'd got a mile along the river. I know the back ways—you don't."

She took down an oilskin jacket from behind the door and tossed it to him together with an old peaked cap. "Ready when you are."

She picked up her hunting rifle and led the way

out through the front door and down towards the river. There was still no boat moored at the little wooden jetty. She passed it, moving through dense undergrowth and emerged on to a small cleared bank which dropped cleanly into the water. Her boat, a flat bottomed marsh punt with an old motor attached to the stern, was tied to a tree.

Chavasse cast off while she busied herself with the motor. As it coughed into life, he pushed the punt through the encircling reeds and stepped in.

Liri Kupi certainly knew what she was doing. At one point, they hit rough water where the river twisted round sandbanks, spilling across ragged rocks, and she handled the frail craft like an expert, swinging the tiller at just the right moment to sweep them away from the worst hazards.

After a while, they left the Buene, turning into a narrow creek which circled through a great stagnant swamp, losing itself among a hundred lagoons and waterways.

When they finally came into the river again, it was in the lee of a large island. The mist hung like a grey curtain from bank to bank, and as they moved from the shelter of the island to cross over, he could smell woodsmoke and somewhere a dog barked.

The first houses loomed out of the mist, scattered along one side of the river and Liri took the punt in close. She produced the tin of cigarettes from her pocket and threw it to Chavasse.

"Better have one. Try to look at home."

"Home was never like this."

He lit a cigarette, leaned back against the prow and watched the town unfold itself. There were fewer than five hundred inhabitants these days, that much he knew. Since the cold war had warmed up between Yugoslavia and Albania, the river traffic had almost stopped and the Buene was now so silted up as to be unnavigable for boats of any size.

The monastery lifted out of the mist, a vast sprawling mediaeval structure with crumbling walls, several hundred yards back from the river bank.

The Albanian flag, hanging limply in the rain, lifted in a gust of wind, the red star standing out vividly against the black, double-headed eagle, and a bugle sounded faintly.

A little further along the bank, forty or fifty convicts worked, some of them waist deep in water as they drove in the piles for a new jetty. Chavasse noticed that the ones on the banks had their ankles chained together.

"Politicals," Liri said briefly. "They send them here from all over the country. They don't last long in the marshes when the hot weather comes."

She eased the tiller, turning the punt in towards the bank and a small ruined chapel whose crumbling walls fell straight into the river. At the foot of the wall, the entrance to a narrow tunnel gaped darkly and Liri took the punt inside.

There was a good six feet of headroom and Chavasse reached out to touch cold, damp walls, straining his eyes into the darkness which suddenly lightened considerably. Liri cut the motor and the punt drifted in towards a landing stage constructed of large blocks of worked masonry.

They scraped beside a flight of stone steps and Chavasse tied up to an iron ring and handed her out. Light filtered down from somewhere above and she smiled through the half darkness.

"I shan't be long."

She mounted a flight of stone steps and Chavasse lit another cigarette, sat on the edge of the jetty and waited. She was gone for at least fifteen minutes. When she returned, she didn't come all the way down, but called to him from the top of the steps.

He went up quickly and she turned, opened a large oak door and led the way along a narrow passage. She opened another door at the far end and they stepped into the interior of the small chapel.

The lights were very dim and, down by the altar, the candles flickered and the Holy Mother was bathed in light. The smell of incense was overpowering and Chavasse felt a little giddy. It was a long time since he had been in church, too long as his mother was never tired of reminding him, and he smiled wryly as they moved down the aisle.

Father Shedu knelt in prayer at the altar, the brown habit dark and sombre in the candlelight. His eyes were closed, the worn face completely calm, and somehow, the ugly puckered scar of the old bullet wound which had carried away the left eye seemed completely in character.

He was a man, strong in his faith, certain in his knowledge of that which was ultimately important.

Men like Enver Hoxha and Adem Kapo would come and go, ultimately to break upon the rock that was Father Shedu.

He crossed himself, got to his feet in one smooth movement and turned to face them. Chavasse suddenly felt awkward under the keen scrutiny of that single eye. For a moment, he was a little boy again at his grandfather's village in Finistère just after the war when France was free again, standing before the old, implacable parish priest, trying to explain his absence from mass, the tongue drying in his mouth.

Father Shedu smiled and held out his hand. "I am happy to meet you, my son. Liri has told me something of why you are here."

Chavasse shook hands, relief flowing through him. "She seemed to think you might be able to help, Father."

"I know something of what happened to the statue of Our Lady of Scutari," the priest said. "It was my predecessor, Father Kupescu, who gave it into the charge of the young man who was later killed in the marshes. Father Kupescu has since paid for his actions with his life, I might add."

"The girl who was with me was the young man's sister," Chavasse said. "She was the one who guided us to the position of Minetti's launch."

Father Shedu nodded. "She and an Italian named Orsini arrived in Tama earlier this afternoon. They were taken to the monastery."

"Are you sure?"

"I was visiting sick prisoners at the time, one of the little privileges I still insist on."

"I'm surprised you're allowed to function at all."

Father Shedu smiled faintly. "As you may have noticed, my name is the same as that of our beloved President, something for which the average party member holds me in superstitious awe. They can never be quite sure that I'm not some kind of third cousin, you see. There are things they can do, of course. We had a wonderful old church here. Now, it's a restaurant. They use the altar as a counter and the nave is crammed with tables at which the happy workers can consume *kebab* and *shashlik* to the greater glory of Enver Hoxha."

"All things in their own good time, Father," Chavasse said.

The priest smiled. "As it happens, I *can* help you, Mr. Chavasse. Your friends are at the moment imprisoned in the back guardroom which is inside the inner wall of the monastery. A Colonel of Intelligence and a high *sigurmi* official named Kapo, who brought them in, left again almost at once with every spare soldier they could lay their hands on."

"To look for me."

"Obviously. I shouldn't think there will be more than one man on duty at the guardroom—perhaps two."

"But how could we get in, Father?" Liri demanded. "There are two walls to pass through and guards on each gate."

"We go under, my dear. It's really quite simple. The good fathers who built this monastery thought of everything. Come with me."

He led the way out of the chapel and back along

the passage to the door which led down to the landing stage. He took an electric torch from a ledge on which an ikon stood and went down to the water's edge. When he switched on the torch, its beam splayed against the rough walls of the tunnel which ran on into the darkness, narrowing considerably.

"The monastery's underground sewage system comes down through here to empty into the river," he said. "Not a pleasant journey, I'm afraid, but one that will take you inside the walls without being seen."

"Show me the way, that's all I ask, Father," Chavasse said. "You can leave the rest to me."

"To require you not to use violence against violent men would be absurd," Father Shedu said, "but you must understand that I myself could not possibly take part in any such action. You accept this?"

"Willingly."

The priest turned to Liri. "You will stay here, child?"

She shook her head. "There may be a use for me. Please, Father. I know what I'm doing."

He didn't bother to argue, but hitched his trailing robes into the leather belt at his waist and stepped into the water on the left-hand side of the tunnel. It was no more than ankle-deep and Chavasse followed along a broad ledge, his head lowered as the roof dropped to meet them.

There was a strong earthy smell and a slight mist curled from the water, fanning out against the damp roof. The tunnel stretched into the darkness and gradually the water became deeper until he could feel it swirling about his knees.

By now the stench was appalling and he stumbled on, his stomach heaving. Finally, the priest turned into a side passage which came out into a cavern about fifty feet in diameter.

It was some three feet deep in stinking water and at least a dozen tunnels emptied into it. The Franciscan waded across and counted from the left.

"I think the eighth will be the one."

The tunnel was no more than four feet high and Chavasse paused at the entrance and reached out to Liri. "Are you all right?"

"Fine." She chuckled. "The swamps stink worse than this lot in the summer."

They bent double and went after Father Shedu who was now several yards ahead. A few moments later he stopped. Light filtered down through some sort of grille and a short tunnel sloped up towards the surface.

"If I am right," the priest said, "we should be in a cell of the old cloisters behind the square containing the guardhouse."

The tunnel was a good fifty feet in length, the stonework smooth and slippery, making it difficult to climb. The priest went first, Liri next and Chavasse brought up the rear. He jammed himself between the narrow walls, working his way up foot by foot. Once, Liri slipped, falling back against him, but he managed to hold her and they continued.

Above them, Father Shedu was already at the entrance, a large slab which had been carved by some master craftsman into a stone grille. He put his shoulder to it and it slid back easily. He climbed out and turned to give Liri a hand.

Chavasse clambered up after them and found himself in a small crumbling cell with a gaping doorway which opened into half-ruined cloisters, broken pillars lifting into the sky, grass growing between great, cracked stone slabs.

"Through the cloisters and you will come to the square," Father Shedu said. "The guardroom is a small flat-roofed building of brick and concrete." A slight smile touched his mouth. "From here, you are on your own. There is nothing more I can do for you. As I said earlier, I must not play any active part in this affair. I will wait here." He turned to Liri. "You will stay with me?"

She shook her head stubbornly. "There may be something I can do. Something to help."

"Father Shedu's right," Chavasse said. "You stay."

"If you want my gun, then you take me." She patted the stock of the old hunting rifle. "That's my final word."

Chavasse looked at the priest who sighed heavily. "A will of iron, I'm afraid, and she hates the Reds."

Chavasse said to Liri, "You can come as far as the edge of the square. You watch from there while I go in. If anything goes wrong, you'll have plenty of time to join Father Shedu and get clear. All right?"

He moved out across the ruined courtyard and through the cloisters to the crumbling wall on the far side. The square stretched before him, quiet and still. The guardhouse was built against the wall half way along the other side, just as Father Shedu had described, a difficult place to come at from the front.

In the far wall, great double gates leading to the outer square were closed.

Chavasse turned to Liri. "You stay here, I'm going to work my way round the wall so that I come in from the other side where there's no windows. If anything happens, get out of it fast and back to Father Shedu." She started to protest, but he pulled the rifle firmly from her grasp. "Now be a good girl and do as you're told."

He moved along behind the ruined wall to the point where it joined the other, stepped into the open and ran, half-crouching, until he reached the side of the guardhouse. He paused, conscious of the sweat soaking his shirt, and started forward. At that moment the guardhouse door opened and someone stepped out.

Chavasse heard voices, two men talking. One of them laughed and a match was struck. He was trapped with no place to run. If one of them took a step to the corner of the building, he was certain to be discovered.

A fresh young voice called, "Heh, you there! Yes, you, you great ox. Come here!"

Liri Kupi strolled calmly across the square, her hands in her pockets. Her intention was obviously to attract the attention of the guards and she succeeded perfectly. As Chavasse went along the side of the guardhouse, two soldiers moved out to meet Liri.

They weren't even armed and one of them was stripped to the waist as if he had been having a wash. Chavasse ran forward, raised the rifle and rammed it down hard against an exposed neck. As the soldier crumpled with a groan, the other swung round. Chavasse swung the barrel viciously into the man's stomach. He gave a sort of strangled scream and keeled over, and the butt of the rifle smashed his skull.

Chavasse was already moving towards the door when Liri arrived on the run, her face flushed. "There can't be anyone else. They'd have come out when I called."

"Let's hope you're right."

The outer office was quiet, papers scattering across the desk in the wind which blew in through the doorway. Keys hung on a board on the far wall. Chavasse moved across quickly and opened the inner door. There were only six cells. The first four were empty. Guilio Orsini was in the fifth, sprawled on a narrow bunk, head on hands.

"Now then, you old bastard," Chavasse said amiably.

The Italian sat up, an expression of astonishment on his face. He jumped on his feet and crossed to the grille. "Paul, by all that's holy! You go in for miracles now?"

"Ask and ye shall receive," Chavasse said. "You'll never know just how apt that quotation is. Where's Francesca?"

"Next door. We've been here ever since we arrived. Kapo took off again in something of a hurry. Presumably to chase you."

"He's out of luck."

Liri was beside him with the keys. As she released Orsini, Chavasse was already at the next grille. Francesca Minetti stood there, eyes like dark holes in the white face.

"I knew you'd come, Paul."

He took the keys from Liri and unlocked the cell. Francesca came straight into his arms. He held her close for a moment, then pushed her away.

"We've got to get moving."

Orsini was already ahead of them, following Liri, and Chavasse picked up the rifle and pushed Francesca along the passage. The Italian paused in the doorway and looked out into the square.

"Seems quiet enough."

The noise of the siren rising through the still air was like a physical blow, numbing the senses. Chavasse swung round and saw Francesca on the other side of the room. She had opened a small metal box on the wall and her thumb was pressed firmly against a scarlet button.

He pulled her away so violently that she staggered back against the desk. "What the hell are you playing at?"

She spat in his face and slapped him heavily across the left cheek and in an instinctive reflex action, he returned the blow with his clenched fist, knocking her to the floor.

She lay there moaning softly and Orsini grabbed Chavasse by the sleeve, pulling him round, "For God's sake, what's going on?"

A single shot echoed across the square, splintering the doorpost and Orsini ducked, pulling Liri to the floor. Chavasse looked out through the window and saw a movement on the wall above the great gates.

Another rifle shot was followed by the rapid stutter of a sub machine gun and a line of bullets kicked a cloud of dust into the air in a brown curtain.

He smashed the window with the butt end of the hunting rifle, aimed quickly and fired. There was a faint cry and a soldier pitched over the parapet and fell, still clutching his rifle.

One of the two guards lying in the square pushed himself on to his knees, an expression of bewilderment on his face. Chavasse shot him through the head and ducked out of sight as the man's comrades started to concentrate on the window.

He moved to the doorway and crouched beside Orsini and the girl. "There must be half a dozen of them up there now and more on the way. I'm going to draw their fire. It might give you and Liri a chance. She knows the way. Just do as she says."

Orsini opened his mouth to protest, but Chavasse was already running into the square. He flung himself down beside the body of the guard he had shot, took aim and started to fire at the men on the wall.

Behind him, Orsini and the girl emerged from the guardhouse and started to run. It was at precisely that moment that the great double doors on the far side of the square swung open. An engine burst into life and a jeep roared through in a cloud of dust. A light machine gun was mounted on a swivel in the rear and Colonel Tashko swung it in a half arc, a line of bullets churning the dust into fountains beside Orsini and the girl, bringing them to a halt, hands held high.

Chavasse, the heart freezing inside him, saw a

detail of soldiers come through the gate, rifles at the port. In the moment that the jeep braked, slewing broadside on, Francesca staggered past him and lurched towards it. Chavasse jumped to his feet and fired the hunting rifle from the hip as he ran.

His first shot kicked up dirt a foot to one side of her and then something punched him in the left arm, spinning him round, the rifle flying from his grasp. He crouched like an animal, holding his arm tightly, blood oozing between the fingers and heard boots crunch through the dirt in the sudden silence.

When he raised his eyes, Adem Kapo looked down at him, a slight smile fixed to the small mouth.

11

light on the situation

Rain drifted in through the bars of the window and Chavasse pulled himself up and looked out across the monastery walls towards the river. He was immediately aware of the pain in his left arm and dropped with a curse.

The bullet had passed through cleanly, a simple flesh wound and the only treatment he had so far received was to have it roughly bandaged. They were in some sort of storeroom on the second floor of the main building and Liri Kupi slept in the corner, a blanket hitched over her shoulders.

Orsini crouched beside her to straighten the blanket. When he rose to his feet there was a strange expression on his face. "Quite a girl. A pity she had to get mixed up in a thing like this."

"As I've already explained, she wasn't supposed to." Chavasse walked to the door, peered through

115

the grille at the guard outside. "God, what a fool I've been. It stuck out like a sore thumb and I never saw it."

"Francesca?" Orsini shook his head. "I still can't believe it."

"She said the Madonna was in the forward cabin and it wasn't and remember we had to blast our way in. How do you get round that?" He kicked a packing case savagely. "The little bitch. That night outside the *Tabu* when she was attacked. They must have been waiting for me to show. The whole thing was laid on for my benefit."

"But why?" Orsini demanded. "It doesn't make sense. And what happened to the Madonna?"

"That's one thing I'd like to know myself. That part of the story was genuine enough, because Father Shedu confirmed it. At least they don't seem to have laid hands on him, which is a good thing."

A key rattled in the lock and the door was flung open. Liri came awake and scrambled to her feet as two soldiers moved into the room followed by Tashko. He examined the girl and smiled.

"I'll come to you later."

She spat in his face and he reached out, quick as a snake, and grabbed her shoulder. As Orsini and Chavasse started forward, the soldiers raised their machine pistols threateningly.

Tashko's face was quite expressionless as his thumb expertly pressed a nerve against bone. Liri's mouth opened in a soundless cry and she crumpled to the floor. He turned to Chavasse, adjusting his leather gloves.

"*Karate*, my friend. Perhaps you've heard of it? You were lucky with that vodka bottle. Next time, all the luck will be mine—this I promise you."

He nodded and one of the soldiers grabbed Chavasse by the shoulder and dragged him outside. He had a quick glimpse of Orsini dropping to one knee beside the girl and then the door closed.

They took him along the wide stone-flagged passage and up a narrow circular staircase at the far end. Tashko opened a door at the top and led the way into a comfortably furnished office.

Adem Kapo sat behind a desk, reading through some papers. He glanced up and a smile flashed across his face. "You'll never know just how much of a pleasure this is. We've been most anxious to lay hands on you since that little affair in Tirana the other week."

"*Sigurmi?*"

Kapo nodded. "My Italian front is only one of the numerous facets of my personality as I'm sure you'll appreciate."

"Oh, I do," Chavasse said. "But what about a few answers? Only sporting and all that."

"But of course." Kapo smiled jovially. "The English side of your nature coming out I presume?"

"The business in Matano? It was all a fix? No Ramiz? No Marco Minetti?"

"Ramiz was just a little blood on the floor and a substantial bribe to a young woman who lived just across the hall from his room. Minetti was a figment of the imagination."

"Which explains why Francesca was so insistent

that I didn't disclose what was going on to s2 Headquarters in Rome?"

Kapo nodded. "The story was genuine enough. It was played out by a rather high-minded young Italian named Carveggio who tried the same trick and got his head blown off for his pains."

"And the statue?"

"We recovered it from the wreck almost immediately."

He nodded to Tashko who went to a cupboard, opened it and took out a shapeless bundle. He unwrapped a grey blanket and set the statue on the desk.

She was perhaps four feet high and carved from a single piece of ebony, her robes inlaid with gold. The features carried an expression of wonderful serenity and peace. A supreme achievement by some great artist.

"All right," Chavasse said. "In all essential details, the story handed me by Francesca Minetti was true and it did what it was supposed to do—got me back into Albania. Which means you went to a hell of a lot of trouble—why?"

Kapo selected a cigarette from a wooden box on the desk and leaned back in his chair. "As you may know, relations between my own poor country and the U.S.S.R. and its satellites have somewhat deteriorated over the past few years. In our trouble, only one friend came to our aid—China."

"How touching."

"We are a sentimental people, I assure you. We like to pay our debts. The report from our counterintelligence section, which contained the information that you intended to enter our country as a member of an Italian workers' holiday group, was passed on to Chinese Intelligence Headquarters in Tirana as a matter of courtesy. They expressed great interest. Apparently you did them some dis-service in Tibet last year. Something to do with a Doctor Hoffner, I understand. We promised to let them have you."

"And then I slipped through your fingers."

"But not for long, you must agree, and thanks to only one person. An extremely able member of the counter-intelligence section of the *sigurmi*. Perhaps you'd like to meet her?"

When Tashko opened the door she came in at once. She was still in the clothes she had worn on the boat, but looked different. Harder, more assured.

"Why, Francesca, why?" he said.

"I am as much Albanian as I am Italian," she said calmly. "One can't have a foot in both worlds. I chose mine long ago."

"You mean you've been working for the other side ever since s2 took you on?"

"How else did you think our people in Tirana knew you were coming? I only transmitted that radio warning from Scutari because the night duty officer was present when it came in."

And then it really hit him for the first time like a kick in the guts. At the very heart of things, with a top security rating, someone from the other side had been sitting for two years, passing on the information men had sweated and died for, perhaps even sending them to their deaths.

Something of this must have shown on his face

and she smiled slightly. "Oh, yes, Paul, I have accomplished great things. Remember Matt Sorley and the Frenchman, Dumont? Neither of them lasted long, I saw to that. And there were others."

"You lousy bitch."

"You killed my husband, Paul," she said calmly and a cold hatred blazed from her eyes.

"Your husband?" He frowned slightly and shook his head. "I don't know what you're talking about. In any case, I've seen your personal file. There was no mention of any marriage."

"Not a difficult thing to keep quiet about if one goes the right way about it. His name was Enrico Noci. You drowned him like a rat in a fishing net. No marks, no violence. Just an accident."

"Which I must say was really damned ingenious of you," Kapo put in.

There was obviously nothing more to say and Chavasse turned from her to the little man. "What happens now? A quick flight to Peking?"

"No rush." Kapo grinned. "We've all the time in the world and there's so much you could tell me. How on earth you managed to get inside the monastery, for example. Of course that was the idea—that you should show up. We were quite certain that a man of your resource and energy wouldn't leave his friends in the lurch, but to be perfectly honest, your sudden materialization out of thin air was even more than I'd reckoned on."

"A trick I picked up from an old *fakir* in India years ago."

"Fascinating. You can tell me all about it when I

return. If you can't, I'm sure Tashko can persuade the young lady you picked up on your travels to be more co-operative."

Chavasse ignored the veiled threat and calmly helped himself to a cigarette from the box on the desk. "You're going somewhere?"

"Didn't I explain?" Kapo took another cigarette, lit it and tossed the matches across to Chavasse. They might have been good friends enjoying a pleasant conversation. "It's really rather ingenious, though I do say it myself. At the moment, your young friend Arezzo is sitting on the *Buona Esperanza* awaiting your return."

Which didn't make sense at all. Chavasse was unable to suppress a slight frown and Kapo smiled. "Later tonight, I shall take Francesca in the motor boat to within a reasonable distance of the launch. In the grey light of dawn, she will float out of the mist in your dinghy, in a distressed condition, I might add."

"And with an even more distressing story to tell."

"But of course. They'll be most upset back at s2 when they hear they've lost the gallant Chavasse and his friend Orsini."

"And you think they'll accept Francesca back into the fold without a question?" Chavasse shook his head. "My boss has a mind like a sewer. He'll check every step she's taken since she was six months old."

"I wouldn't be too sure." Kapo smiled. "You see she'll have the Black Madonna with her, such a lovely stroke of propaganda against Albania. Everyone will be so pleased."

And he was right. It was good. Damned good. Kapo started to laugh and nodded to Tashko. "Take him back to his friends. I'll deal with him when I return in the morning."

Chavasse turned to face Francesca. She held his gaze for a moment, then looked away and Tashko gave him a push towards the door. They went down the stairs and back along the corridor.

Just before they reached the storeroom again, Tashko paused to light a long Russian cigarette. The two soldiers waited respectfully a few paces away, obviously frightened to death of him and he glared at Chavasse coldly.

"That one up there is a big man with words, but I have a different approach. Soon you will find this out."

"Why don't you take a running jump," Chavasse said calmly.

Rage flared in the cold eyes. Tashko took a step forward and restrained himself with obvious difficulty. There was the door to another room to one side of Chavasse and, quite suddenly, the Albanian's right fist shot forward in a straight line in that terrible basic *karate* blow known as the reverse punch. The inch thick centre plank of the door splintered and sagged inwards.

There was a little Japanese professor whose class Chavasse attended three times a week whenever he was in London, who could do the same thing to three planks at once and he was half Tashko's size. His words echoed faintly like an old tune: *Science, Cha-*

vasse San. Science, not force. God did not intend the brute to lord it over earth.

"Try to imagine what that would have done to your face," Tashko said.

"It's certainly a thought."

Chavasse moved on along the passage holding his own counsel. One of the soldiers unlocked the door and they pushed him inside. As it closed, he looked through the grille into Tashko's cold eyes.

The Albanian nodded. "Don't worry. I'll be back."

His footsteps died along the corridor and Chavasse turned to the others. Orsini was sitting by the window, an arm around Liri and the blanket was draped over their shoulders. It was bitterly cold.

"What happened?" Orsini demanded.

Chavasse told him. When he had finished, Liri shook her head. "She must be a devil, that one."

"No, *cara,* no devil," Orsini said. "She is like all her kind, convinced that she alone knows the ultimate truth of things. To achieve it, she believes anything to be permissible."

"Which doesn't help any of us one little bit," Chavasse said.

He went and sat on a packing case, turning up the collar of his jacket, and folded his arms to conserve what heat was left in his body, thinking about Francesca Minetti. So Enrico Noci had been her husband? Strange that a woman so obviously intelligent should fall for that sort of man. It only went to show just how unreliable women were where this sort of thing was concerned. Too much a prey to their emotions.

Orsini and Liri were talking together in low voices,

a strange intimacy between them. What was it someone had once said? A day told you as much about a person as ten years? Pity they'd had to meet under such circumstances.

How ironic that Guilio Orsini, the man who had penetrated the main harbour at Alexandria on one of the first underwater chariots, who had sunk two British destroyers, survivor of one desperate exploit after the other through the years, should end like this because he had been touched by the apparent sorrow of a young girl. Life could be strangely puzzling. After a while, his head dropped forward on his breast and he slept.

12

the sound of violence

He was not certain of what had caused him to awaken and lay for a moment, staring through the darkness, conscious of the ache in his cramped muscles, of the bitter cold. His watch was still functioning and the luminous dial told him that it was two a.m. He sat there for a moment, aware of the wind howling across the square outside, and got to his feet.

There was movement in the corridor and when he looked out through the grille he could see the sentry standing in front of his chair, a look of abject terror on his face. Colonel Tashko confronted him, hands on hips.

"So, you were sleeping, you worm."

His hand lashed forward, catching the unfortunate sentry across the side of the face, sending him back across his chair with a crash. As the man scrambled to his feet, Tashko booted him along the corridor.

"Go on, get out of it! Report to the guardhouse. I'll deal with you later."

Orsini and Liri, awakened by the disturbance, came to the door. "What is it?" Orsini demanded.

"Tashko," Chavasse told him briefly. "I think he's drunk."

The Albanian moved to the door and looked through the grille at Chavasse, a strange expression in his eyes. His tunic hung open and underneath he was naked to the waist, great muscles standing out like cords.

He unbuckled the black leather holster at his hip and took out a Mauser, then unlocked the door and opened it slowly. They could smell the liquor on his breath, heavy and penetrating and Liri took an involuntary step towards Orsini whose arm encircled her at once.

"How touching," Tashko sneered.

"It's been a long day and we'd like to get a little sleep," Chavasse said. "So kindly state your business and get to hell out of here."

"Still full of fight?" Tashko said. "That's the way I like it. Let's have you outside."

"And what if I tell you to go to hell?"

"I shoot the girl through her left kneecap. A pity to waste good material, but there it is."

Orsini took a step forward, but Chavasse pushed him back. "Leave it, Guilio. My affair." He moved into the corridor and Tashko slammed the door and locked it. "I don't think Kapo's going to like this. He's saving me for Peking."

"To hell with Peking," Tashko said. "In any case,

I'm in charge now. Kapo and the girl left half an hour ago."

He sent Chavasse staggering along the corridor with a powerful shove and followed three feet behind, the Mauser ready for action. They went down a spiral staircase at the far end, turned along a broad stone passage and descended a flight of stone steps that seemed to go down forever.

At the bottom, Tashko produced his keys and unlocked an oaken door, stoutly bound with bands of iron. Chavasse moved in and Tashko flicked a switch and locked the door behind them.

They stood at the top of a flight of broad stone steps and beneath them in the dim light of a couple of electric bulbs was an amazing sight. A great Roman plunge bath, perhaps a hundred feet long, stretched into the gloom flanked by broken pillars and the stumps of what must have been at one time well proportioned colonnades. There was a strong sulphurous smell and steam drifted up from the water.

"Amazing what they got up to, the Romans," Tashko said. "Of course the mediaeval fathers who built this monastery weren't too keen on such pagan survivals. They simply built over it."

They went down the steps and crossed a cracked tessellated floor. The pool was about six feet deep, the water very still and the face in the brightly coloured mosaic that was its floor gazed blindly up at him out of two thousand years of chaos.

"It's fed by a natural spring," Tashko said. "120 degrees Fahrenheit. Quite pleasant. They say it's good for rheumatism."

As Chavasse turned slowly, the Albanian slipped off his tunic and let it drop to the floor. He held up the keys in one hand, the Mauser in the other, then tossed them into the centre of the pool with a quick gesture.

"Nothing to help you this time, my friend."

So that was it? Quite simply, a case of personal vanity on the part of a man so proud of his brute strength that he couldn't bear to be beaten by anyone. Chavasse stumbled back as if panic-stricken. If Tashko thought him an easy mark, he might still do something stupid.

The Albanian moved forward, arms at his side, and laughed harshly. In the same moment he delivered a tremendous reverse punch, the basic *karate* blow which takes the uninitiated unawares because it is delivered with the hand which is on the same side as the rear foot.

Chavasse crossed his hands above his head to counter with the X-block, the famous *juji-uke*, and delivered a forward elbow strike in return that caught Tashko full in the mouth, splintering his teeth like matchwood.

The Albanian staggered back, blood spurting from his crushed lips and Chavasse grinned. "A *gyaku-zuki* and badly delivered. Is that the best you can do?"

Tashko's face was twisted by anger, but he immediately dropped into the defensive position, adopting the cat stance, arms down inviting combat. Chavasse moved in, his right forearm vertical, the left protecting his body. They circled warily and Tashko made the first move.

He pushed the heel of his palm at his opponent's face and as Chavasse blocked it, delivered a lightning punch to the stomach. Chavasse turned sideways, riding most of the force and at the same moment, fell to one side and delivered a roundhouse kick to the groin. The Albanian keeled over and Chavasse, throwing caution to the winds, raised a knee into the descending face.

He realized immediately that he had made a bad mistake. A blow which would have demolished any ordinary man only succeeding in shaking the Albanian's massive strength and great hands clawed across his body, grabbing for his throat.

The lights seemed to be very far away and there was sudden roaring in his ears and through it he seemed to hear the professor's monotonous, sing-song voice. *Science—science and intelligence will beat brute force.*

He summoned every effort of will-power and spat full in that great stinking face and Tashko recoiled in a reflex action that was as natural as breathing. Chavasse stabbed upwards with stiffened fingers at the exposed throat and Tashko screamed and staggered back.

Chavasse rolled over several times and came to his feet as the big man lurched towards him, hands extended, all science forgotten. Chavasse ducked in under the hands, delivering a fore-fist punch, knuckles extended and it sank into the muscles beneath Tashko's rib-cage. He started to fall and Chavasse raised his knee into the descending face, throwing him back.

Tashko swayed on the edge of the pool, his face a mask of blood and Chavasse jumped high in the air, delivering a flying front kick, the devastating *mae-tobigeri*, into the Albanian's face, knocking him back into the water.

Chavasse followed him in, twisting in mid-air, going under awkwardly, the warm water drawing him down. His hands took the shock against a bearded mosaic face and he surfaced quickly.

Tashko was about twenty feet away, lurching towards the centre of the pool where he had thrown the Mauser and Chavasse went after him. He scrambled up on to the great back, his hands sliding under the armpits, locking together at the nape of the neck. He started to press and Tashko screamed. All pity dying in him, Chavasse maintained that relentless pressure and the great head sank down into the water.

The body bucked and heaved, hands flailing the surface into a cauldron, but Chavasse strengthened his grip and hung on. The end came with startling suddenness. Tashko simply went limp and when Chavasse released his grip, planed down through the water, turning on his back when he reached bottom.

Chavasse took a quick breath and went after the Mauser. The keys were perhaps ten feet away and he had to push Tashko to one side to pick them up. The Albanian's eyes stared into eternity, blood drifting in brown strings from his smashed face and Chavasse turned and swam for the side.

He sat on the edge for perhaps five minutes, his chest heaving, drawing air into his tortured lungs.

When he felt a little better, he got to his feet and mounted the steps. He had to try four keys before he found the right one. As he opened the door, he looked down for the last time at Tashko who stared up at him, just another figure in the mosaic now. He switched off the lights, closed the door and locked it.

The corridors were quiet and he met no one on his way back. Outside the storeroom, the chair on which the sentry had been sleeping still lay on its side and he righted it before slipping the Mauser into his pocket and fumbling with the keys.

As he worked through them, Guilio Orsini appeared at the grille. He glanced up and down the passage and an expression of bewilderment appeared on his face.

"What happened to Tashko?"

"He made a mistake," Chavasse said, swinging the door open. "His last. Let's get going."

He turned along the passage, remembering the way they had come. A stone spiral staircase dropped to the first floor, another to the basement. All was quiet and he led the way along a narrow whitewashed corridor, pausing to reconnoitre the entrance hall at the end. There was no sentry, but then, why should there be? The building was encircled by two thirty foot walls, the main gates in each being strongly guarded.

They had explained earlier to Orsini how they had gained access to the monastery and the big Italian followed Chavasse unhesitatingly, the girl at his side.

They kept to the shadow of the wall, skirting the square on the far side of the guardhouse where a light shone in the window and entered the cloisters through a gap in the ruined wall. It was very dark and Chavasse moved through the pillars cautiously and turned into the passage containing the cells.

He had to try three before he found one with the grille and it was Orsini who pulled it out, great fingers fastening into the latticework like steel hooks.

"I'll go first," Chavasse said. "Then Liri. You follow Guilio, and replace the grille as you come down."

He shot down the stone chute on his back, forearms raised to protect his face and landed in the tunnel below with a splash. Liri followed so quickly that she cannoned into him as he was getting to his feet. Orsini joined them a moment later and they crouched in a little group.

It was so dark in the tunnel that they couldn't see each other's faces and Chavasse said quietly, "This isn't going to be any picnic. Whatever happens, keep close together. As long as we can make it to the main channel, we can't go wrong because it's bound to flow in the direction of the river."

"Anything's preferable to what we've just left," Orsini said. "Let's get moving."

Chavasse started along the tunnel bent double, Liri holding on to the tail of his oilskin jacket. It was a strange, claustrophobic sensation, like nothing he had ever experienced before and yet he wasn't frightened. The darkness was a friend, cloaking their flight, enfolding them in gentle hands and he was grateful.

A few moments later they emerged from the tunnel

into the central cavern. He stood thigh deep in the stinking water, staring into the darkness.

"Father Shedu counted eight openings to the left from where we came out, Paul," Liri said.

He nodded. "Keep behind me, both of you. I've got an idea."

He took out the Mauser, pointed it at the water and fired. In the single brilliant flash of light, the tunnel openings stood out like dark wounds. He fired again, counting quickly, then started across the pool. His questing hand found the opening and he grunted.

Fifty yards further on, the passage emptied itself into the main tunnel and he could hear the splash and gurgling of the water on its way down to the river. Already the stench seemed to be lessening and as he followed the wall, Chavasse breathed deeply to clear the heaviness that weighed upon his brain.

The landing stage loomed out of the darkness, light flowing down from the candles burning at the ikon in the niche at the head of the stairs. Liri's punt was still tied to the bottom of the steps and Chavasse sat on the edge of the landing stage and rubbed the back of one hand wearily across his eyes.

"How much juice you got in that thing? Enough to get us to the coast?"

"I think so. Most of the way, at least."

"We still need a compass to get back to the *Buona Esperanza*," Orsini said. "At least if we're going to go now in the dark."

"We can't afford to wait till dawn," Chavasse said.

"That's when Kapo will send Francesca in the dinghy. If we're going to beat them to it, we must go now."

"Father Shedu will have a compass," Liri said. "Wait here. I'll go and get him."

She mounted the steps and the door closed behind her. Orsini slumped down beside Chavasse. "What a girl! Most would have had hysterics by now."

"She'll have to come with us," Chavasse said. "She can't stay here now."

"What about an entry permit? I know what it's like for the stateless refugees."

"Don't worry about that. I know the right people at the Ministry at Rome. I'll see she gets treated like royalty. We'll even find her a job. She's earned it."

"Maybe she won't need a job."

Chavasse glanced at him curiously. "You make up your mind in a hurry, don't you?"

Orsini shrugged. "You either know straight away, or it's no good. Of course, I've got twenty years on her."

"I wouldn't let that worry you," Chavasse said. "She knows a man when she sees one."

He sat there, his left arm aching like hell, his strength slowly ebbing and after a while, the door clicked open and Father Shedu came down the steps with Liri.

"So miracles can still happen," he said as he moved forward.

"My friend, Guilio Orsini, Father," Chavasse said. "I'm glad you kept out of it back there. They still haven't got the slightest idea how we got inside."

The priest poured brandy into a couple of tin mugs and handed a small basket to Liri. "Not much, I'm afraid. Bread and cheese and some dried meat. The rich, full life is long in coming for the People's Republic."

"We'll eat it on the way," Chavasse said.

He drank some of the brandy and coughed as it burned its way down his throat. "Liri has told me what happened in there," the priest said. "It pains me to know this woman deceived you."

"And she'll go on playing the same game unless we can manage to stop her," Chavasse said. "Liri thought you might have a compass?"

The priest held one forward, pressing a small spring so that the lid flew open. Chavasse examined it, noting the inscription w.d. 1941 and the official broad arrow.

"British Army issue?"

"A souvenir from another life. Take it with my blessing." He turned to Liri and placed a hand on her shoulder. "And what happens to you, Liri?"

"She goes with us, Father," Orsini said gruffly. "I'll look after her."

The priest gazed at him searchingly and then smiled. "God moves in His own strange ways. Now go, all of you, while there is still time."

They dropped into the boat and Liri took the tiller. The roaring of the engine seemed to fill the cavern when it broke into life and the boat turned away quickly.

As they moved through the dark entrance, Chavasse glanced back and saw the Franciscan still standing there watching them. A moment later, they swung into the main current and turned downstream through the darkness.

13

action by night

The river was angry, swollen by the rains flowing down from the mountains of the north and it rushed towards the sea with more than usual force.

The frail punt skipped water constantly and Chavasse and Orsini took turns at bailing with an old tin basin. They ate the food the priest had provided and finished the bottle of brandy.

Chavasse sat in the prow, his collar turned up against the spray, and longed for a cigarette. He wondered what Kapo would do? Probably tie up further downriver till dawn. Then he would send Francesca in with the dinghy and Carlo would swallow every damned thing she said.

Perhaps half an hour later, the engine faltered and died abruptly. As the punt started to drift broadside on in the strong current, Liri called, "There are paddles under the seat. Keep her head round."

Chavasse fumbled in the darkness and found two crude paddles. He leaned over the side and dug one deep into the water, using all his strength and gradually the punt turned into the current.

Orsini scrambled to the stern and, after a struggle, managed to get the engine housing off. He started to try to trace the fault by touch alone and after a while his sensitive fingers encountered a broken lead to one of the plugs. The wire was old and brittle and crumbled between his fingers, but he eventually managed to link it together and tried the starter. The engine turned over twice, faltered, then rumbled into life and Chavasse rested on the thwart in relief as the punt surged forward.

"Any chance of that happening again?" he called softly.

"I wouldn't be surprised. This must be the one they used on the Ark."

Orsini stayed at the tiller, nursing the engine along and Liri moved into the centre and started to bail. It was still quite dark and visibility was almost nil. Only the surge of white water against the bank gave them any kind of bearing.

The bulk of a large island loomed out of the night and she called urgently as Orsini swung the tiller, taking them away towards the centre of the river.

As the current caught them, there was a sudden challenge from the left and Chavasse glanced over his shoulder and saw the motor boat anchored in the lee of the island, a light in her wheelhouse.

He was aware of people moving along the deck, of confused voices and then a powerful spot mounted on top of the wheelhouse was switched on, the beam splaying out across the dark water. It followed them relentlessly, trapping them in its dazzling beam like flies in a web.

There was an incredulous cry of dismay and Francesca's voice sounded on the cold air like a bugle. "Kapo! Kapo! Come quickly!"

Chavasse leaned over the side, digging the paddle into the water feverishly as Orsini gave the old motor everything it had. They dipped into the millrace as the current flowed past the final curved point of the island and coasted into darkness again.

A few moments later, the engine of the motor boat rumbled into life and Liri scrambled back into the stern. "I'll take over now," she said. "There's a creek about a quarter of a mile below. If we can reach that, we're safe. It's too narrow for the motor boat to enter. They'll have to stay in the main channel."

Orsini moved down beside Chavasse, picked up the other paddle and drove it into the water with all his great strength. They were passing through a narrower section of the river now and the flood waters rushed with a mighty roar, drowning the sound of the motor boat's engine. Chavasse stabbed the crude paddle into the water again and again, exerting everything of mind and will in a supreme effort, pushing the tiredness, the fatigue, of the past twenty-four hours away from him.

They swung in close to the land as the river broadened, and quite suddenly, as the roaring of the flood waters subsided, the engine of the motor boat sounded close behind.

He glanced over his shoulder, saw the lighted wheelhouse, the searchlight stabbing out towards them. There was the harsh deadly staccato of a sub machine gun and then the punt swerved into the lee of a small island and started to turn.

Reeds swam out of the darkness and as the beam of the searchlight fell across them, the opening of the creek sprang out of the night. The punt surged towards it, slowed as it slid across a submerged mudbank and then they were through. The machine gun rattled again ineffectually as the reeds closed about them.

Liri reduced speed and they coasted on, brushing against the pale fronds. Gradually, the sound of the river faded. The engine of the motor boat had stopped for a while, but now they heard it start again faintly in the distance and fade downstream.

Orsini laughed shakily. "A close call."

Chavasse took from his pocket the compass Father Shedu had given him, and passed it to the Italian. "You'd better start using this. We haven't got time to hang about."

Orsini moved in to the stern beside Liri. "South-southwest must be our general direction. Can we do it?"

"I think so. I know this creek and where it goes. We'll come to a large lagoon soon. We change direction there. But it's possible you might have to get out and push in places."

"When will it be light?" Chavasse asked.

"An hour, perhaps a little longer. It will be misty, one can always tell."

"We're in your hands, *cara*," Orsini told her.

They moved into a large lagoon as she had indicated and turned into a maze of twisting channels. The outboard motor stopped several times as trailing weeds clogged the propeller and finally, it died altogether.

Orsini examined it for several minutes and shook his head. "That's all, I'm afraid. There's nothing I can do, not under these conditions."

From then on they used the paddles and after a while, the reeds became so thick that the two men had to go over the side, wading through thick glutinous mud as they forced a way through for the punt, always trying to keep to their general compass bearing.

The swampy water was treacherous and had a way of changing depth without warning. Once, Chavasse stepped into a deep hole and went in over his head. He struggled back with a curse to a comparatively safe footing and scrambled back into the punt as they emerged into another waterway.

Orsini laughed grimly. "Now this, I could do without."

It was bitterly cold and a damp mist curled from the water. Occasionally, wildfowl fluttered protestingly from the reeds as they passed through, calling angrily to each other, warning those ahead of the intruders.

There was an appreciable lightening of the darkness and a faint luminosity drifted around them. And then they could see the reeds and there was a honking of geese overhead lifting to meet the dawn.

Orsini was pale and drawn, the dark stubble of

his beard accentuating his pallor. He looked about twenty years older, his hands shaking slightly in the extreme cold and Chavasse didn't feel any better. The girl looked healthier than either of them, but on the other hand, she hadn't spent the best part of an hour up to her waist in freezing water.

They coasted into a broad channel and Orsini held up his hand. "We must be close now. Very close."

He stood up in the punt, cupped his hands to his mouth and called at the top of his voice, "*Buona Esperanza*, ahoy! Ahoy, *Buona Esperanza*!"

There was no reply and Chavasse joined him. "Carlo! Carlo Arezzi!"

Their voices died away and in the grey light, they looked helplessly at each other. Liri held up her hand. "I heard something."

At first Chavasse thought it was the cry of a bird, but then it sounded again, unmistakably a human voice. They paddled into the mist, calling again and again and gradually the voice grew louder.

For the last time, Chavasse and Orsini went over the side, forcing the punt through a wall of reeds and then, quite suddenly, they were through and drifting into a familiar lagoon.

At the other end, the *Buona Esperanza* seemed to swim out of the mist to meet them, Carlo Arezzi poised on top of the wheelhouse.

14

breaking through

It was warm in the cabin, Chavasse vigorously rubbed himself down and dressed quickly in a spare pair of denim working pants and a heavy sweater of Carlo's.

There was a knock on the door and Liri Kupi called, "Are you dressed?"

She came in carrying a mug of coffee and he took it gratefully. It was scalding hot and the fragrance seemed to put new life into him. "Best I ever tasted. Where's Guilio?"

"He went up to the wheelhouse. Said something about charting the course."

She opened the little box, gave him one of her Macedonian cigarettes and struck a match for him, holding it in her cupped hands like a man.

Chavasse blew out a cloud of smoke and looked at her shrewdly. "You like him, don't you?"

"Guilio? Who wouldn't?"

"He's got twenty years on you, you know that?"

She shrugged and said calmly, "You know what they say about good wine."

Chavasse chuckled and slipped an arm about her shoulders, giving her a quick squeeze. "You're quite a girl, Liri. I'd say he was a lucky man."

He swallowed the rest of his coffee, handed her the jug and went up the companionway. It started to rain as he went out on deck and the mist draped itself across everything in a grey shroud. Orsini and Carlo were leaning over the charts when he went into the wheelhouse.

"What's the score?" he said.

Orsini shrugged. "I think we should try the main channel out. It's quicker and we could stand a good chance of getting away with it. It's Yugoslavian territory on the other side and Albanian boats don't like going too close. If we can once get into the open, nothing they've got stands a chance of catching us."

"I should have thought Kapo would count on us doing just that."

"He very probably has. I say we go and find out."

Chavasse shrugged. "That's all right by me, but I think it might be an idea to break out a little hardware, just in case."

"You and Carlo can handle that end. I'll get things moving up here."

Chavasse and the young Italian went below, opened the box seat and unpacked the weapons. There was still a sub machine gun left, a dozen grenades and the old Bren. They went back on deck and laid the weapons out on the floor of the wheelhouse under the chart table, ready for action.

It was just after five a.m. when the engines shuddered into life and Orsini took *Buona Esperanza* into the mist. Chavasse stood in the prow beside Liri and rain kicked into his face and the wind, blowing in from the sea, lifted the mist into strange shapes.

The girl stared into the greyness eagerly, lips parted, a touch of colour in each cheek. "Are you glad to be going?" he said.

She shrugged briefly. "I'm leaving nothing behind."

As the light grew stronger, the dark silver lances of the rain became visible, stabbing down through the mist and somewhere a curlew called eerily. Once, twice and he waited with bated breath, trapped by a childhood memory. *Once for joy, two for sorrow, three for a death.*

There was no third call, which left them with a little sorrow, but that he could bear. He turned and went back to the wheelhouse.

For half an hour, they moved slowly along the broad channel, crossing from one lagoon into the other, changing direction only once. Visibility was down to twenty yards, but the reeds were falling away now and the channel was widening.

The water began to kick against the hull in long swelling ripples and Orsini grinned tightly. "The Buene. We're about half a mile from the sea."

The launch crept forward, the engines a low rumble that was almost drowned in the splashing of the heavy rain. Chavasse examined the chart. The estuary was a mass of sandbanks and the main channel, the one which they had used on the way in, was no more than thirty yards. If Kapo was anywhere, it would be there.

A few moments later, Orsini cut the engines and they drifted with the current. He opened the side window and leaned out.

"We're almost there. If they're patrolling, we'll hear the engines."

Chavasse went on deck and stood in the prow listening. Carlo and Liri joined him. At first there was nothing, only the wind and the sizzle of the rain, then Carlo held up a hand.

"I think I hear something."

Chavasse turned, signalling Orsini down and the Italian swung the wheel, taking the boat in to where a low hog's back of sand lifted from the sea. They grounded with a slight shudder and Chavasse ran back to the wheelhouse.

"Carlo thinks he heard something. No sense in running into anything we can avoid. We'll take a look on foot."

He stood on the rail and jumped, landing in a couple of inches of water. Carlo tossed the sub machine gun to him, then followed and they moved into the mist along the sandbank.

It stretched for several hundred yards, in some places water slopping across it so that they had to wade. The noise of an engine was by now quite unmistakable. At times it faded, then a minute or two later grew louder again.

"They must be patrolling the mouth of the channel," Chavasse said.

Carlo pulled him down into the sand. The motor boat floated out of the mist no more than twenty yards away. They had a quick glimpse of a soldier crouching on the roof of the wheelhouse, a machine pistol in his hands, and then the mist swallowed it again.

They ran back along the sandbank and the sound of the motor boat faded behind them. The mist seemed to be a little thicker and the water was rising, flooding in across the dark spine of sand, tugging at their boots as the *Buona Esperanza* loomed out of the gloom.

Chavasse waded into the water and Orsini reached down to give him a hand over the rail. "Are they there?"

Chavasse nodded and explained briefly what they had seen. "What happens now?"

They went back into the wheelhouse and Orsini leaned over the chart. "We could return to the marshes. There is a way through certainly, but it would take many hours with a boat of this size and there is no guarantee. By that time, Kapo could have called in the Albanian Navy, such as it is. They could give us trouble if we ran into them with no way round."

"Have we any choice?"

Orsini traced a finger across the chart. "There's a channel here. It runs a mile to the south west, emerging at Cat Island. See where I mean?"

"What's the snag? It looks good to me."

"As I said earlier, the river isn't used much these days because of the border dispute and channels such as this have been allowed to silt up. There's no knowing just how much water there is any more. Probably shoaled up."

"Are you willing to try?"

"If the rest of you are."

There was really no question, Chavasse knew that as he glanced at Liri, and Orsini pressed the starter and reversed off the sandbank. The launch turned in a long sweeping curve and started back up river.

Orsini leaned out of the side window, eyes narrowed into the mist, and after a while he gave a quick grunt and swung the wheel, taking them between low, humped sandbanks. He reduced speed to dead slow and the boat moved forward as cautiously as an old lady finding her way across a busy street.

Waves slapped hollowly against the bottom, a sure sign of shallow water and once or twice, there was a slight protesting jar and a scraping as they grazed a shoulder of sand. It was perhaps five minutes later that they ploughed to a halt.

Orsini reversed quickly. At first the launch refused to budge and then it parted the sand with an ugly sucking noise. Carlo vaulted over the side without a word to anyone. The water rose to his chest and as he waded forward, it dropped to waist level.

He changed direction to the left and a moment later, it lifted to his armpits again. He waved quickly and Orsini swung the wheel, taking the boat after him.

The young Italian swam forward into the shoals, sounding the bottom every few yards and behind him, *Buona Esperanza* carefully followed his circuitous trail. And then a wave lifted out of the mist, swamping him and he went under.

He surfaced and swam back to the launch and when Chavasse pulled him in, there was a wide grin on his face. "Deep water. I couldn't touch bottom. We're through."

Orsini waved from the wheelhouse and gave the engines more power, swinging the wheel to take them out of the estuary to sea. Fifty yards beyond the entrance, the dark bulk of Cat Island lifted out of the mist and he turned to port. As they rounded the point, the current pushing against them, engines roared into life and a grey naval patrol boat surged out of the rock inlet where she had been waiting.

As she swept across their bows, a heavy machine gun started to fire, bullets sweeping across the deck, shattering glass in the wheelhouse. Chavasse had a quick glimpse of Kapo at the rail, still wearing his hunting jacket with the fur collar, mouth open as he cried his men on.

Carlo appeared in the doorway of the wheelhouse, the sub machine gun at his hip, firing as he crossed the deck to the rail. On the patrol boat, someone screamed and Kapo ducked out of sight.

Already Orsini was taking his engines to full power and from the for'ard deck of the patrol boat another machine gun started to fire, tracer and cannon hammering into the hull of the *Buona Esperanza*, great shudders rushing through her entire frame as she reeled at the impact.

And then they were through, prow lifting over the waves as the patrol boat faded into the mist behind them. Chavasse picked himself up from the deck and gave a hand to Liri. There was blood on her face and she wiped it away quickly.

"Are you all right?" he said.

She nodded. "A flying splinter, that's all."

Carlo turned, the sub machine gun hugged to his breast. For the first time since Chavasse had known him there was a smile on his face.

"I gave one of the bastards something to remember me by."

Chavasse moved to the door of the wheelhouse. The windows were shattered, glass scattered across the floor, but Orsini seemed to be all in one piece.

"I got down quick," he called above the roar of the engine. "Did you see Kapo?"

"For a moment there I thought he'd put one over on us. We should have reckoned on the possibility of him having both exits watched."

"I hope the swine's head rolls for this."

As Orsini grinned savagely, the engines missed a couple of times, faltered, tried to pick up, then stopped completely.

Buona Esperanza ploughed forward, her prow biting into a wave, slowed and started to drift with the current.

15

the last goodbye

When Orsini got the hatch off the tiny engine room, they could smell escaping fuel at once. The Italian slid down the short steel ladder and Chavasse and Orsini followed him.

Carlo made a quick examination and turned. "It could be worse. A section of the fuel intake pipe damaged. We were lucky the whole damned lot didn't blow sky-high."

A jagged hole in the steel hull punched by a cannon shell was mute evidence of how the damage had been caused.

"How are we off for spares?" Orsini demanded.

"No problem there, but I'll have to cut a section to the right size and braze it."

"How long?"

"Twenty minutes if you all get to hell out of here and leave me alone."

Chavasse went up the ladder and joined Liri on deck. "How bad is it?" she said.

"Bad enough to make us sitting ducks for the next half hour."

Orsini scrambled out of the engine room and nodded grimly. "If the swine doesn't get us now, he doesn't deserve to. We'd better make ready, Paul."

He broke open a box of cartridges and carefully loaded the sub machine gun's one hundred round circular clip and Chavasse checked the machine gun and the half dozen magazines which went with it. Liri scrambled on top of the wheelhouse and kept watch, straining her eyes into the mist.

When he had finished loading the sub machine gun Orsini went below and came back with an old American service issue .45 automatic. He tossed it to the girl who caught it deftly.

"Best I can do, but watch it. It has the kick of an angry mule."

"I've been using guns all my life," she said, pulling out the magazine and examining it expertly.

Orsini grinned up at her. "I wonder what you'd look like in a skirt and some decent stockings and shoes. The thought has great appeal. When we reach Matano I must do something about it."

She laughed, her face flushing and then the smile was wiped from her face. "Listen, I think I hear them."

The boat lifted on the swell, waves slapping hollowly against her bows. Chavasse stood at the rail, straining his ears and, in the distance, heard the sound of an engine.

"Come down from there," Orsini told the girl. "Go into the wheelhouse and lie flat."

She had enough sense not to argue and did as she was told. Chavasse stood over her, the barrel of the Bren gun poking through one of the windows and Orsini crouched beside the engine room hatch.

"Perhaps they're going away?" Liri whispered.

Chavasse shook his head. "Not on your life. They must have heard our engines stop and they cut their own and listened to see what was happening. Kapo must know that there are only two possibilities. Either we're being picked up by another boat or our engines have packed in."

The patrol boat came nearer and nearer, obviously beating backwards and forwards through the mist. It passed very close to them indeed, its bow-wave rippling across the water, rocking the *Buona Esperanza* violently. For a moment, Chavasse thought they had been missed and then the engine of the patrol boat lifted and it roared out of the mist.

It swept across their stern and the air was broken by the sound of violence. The main trouble came from the heavy machine gun mounted in the stern of the patrol boat, its crew couched behind a curved shield of armour plating. In the prow, several soldiers stood at the rail firing rifles and machine pistols and Kapo lurked behind them, a revolver in his hand.

Chavasse started to fire, swinging the barrel of the Bren in an arc and a couple of soldiers stumbled backwards to the deck. He saw Francesca running, headdown, and swung the Bren desperately, his bullets chipping the rail beside her head. As his magazine ran out, she disappeared into the wheelhouse.

He ducked, reaching for another magazine and glass shattered above his head and the walls splintered, rocking to the impact of tracer and cannon shell. As the patrol boat swung away, Orsini jumped to his feet and fired a long burst at the crew of the machine gun in the stern. There was a sharp cry. As the boat disappeared into the mist, one of them lurched to the rail and toppled into the sea.

The sound of the patrol boat faded and Orsini shouted to Liri, "Keep down. Next time he's really going to mean business."

The patrol boat circled several times, invisible in the heavy mist, and Chavasse waited impatiently. When Kapo at last made his move it was from a different quarter. As the boat roared out of the mist behind him, Chavasse frantically swung the Bren round, firing from the hip.

The heavy machine gun in the stern of the patrol boat raked them with a murderous fire, the *Buona Esperanza* reeling at the impact and Chavasse ducked as he finished his last magazine and portions of the roof disintegrated above his head.

Orsini was still firing, the barrel of the sub machine gun braced against the side of the wheelhouse. As the patrol boat veered in a wide arc, cutting across their bows again, Chavasse snatched a grenade from the box beside Liri, pulled the pin and ran out on deck.

For a brief moment, the patrol boat was so close that he could see the expression on the soldiers' faces and as it swept by, he lobbed the grenade over the railing to her stern. It started to roll, one of the soldiers kicked out at it frantically and then it exploded. A wave seemed to wash over the stern. When it cleared, only the tangled wreckage of the machine gun was left. The soldiers had vanished.

The patrol boat ran on into the mist and there was quiet. Liri got to her feet, blood on her face, and wiped it away with the back of her hand.

"Will they try again?"

"Certain to. They'll be a little more careful next time, that's all."

Orsini was leaning over the engine room hatch and he stood up and came towards them. "Not so good. At least another fifteen minutes."

They looked at each other without saying anything, knowing what that meant and quite suddenly Kapo's voice boomed out of the mist. "Why don't you give in, Chavasse? You can't hope to get away."

Liri gave a startled exclamation and Orsini reassured her. "Don't be alarmed. He's using a loud hailer, that's all. I wonder what the swine's playing at?"

"Not interested," Chavasse called.

The engines of the patrol boat roared into life and it erupted from the mist, the men at her rail raking the *Buona Esperanza* with small arms fire.

Chavasse shoved Liri down against the deck and Orsini crouched beside them, the sub machine gun chattering angrily. He stopped firing abruptly just as the patrol boat disappeared into the mist.

He checked the magazine, then tossed the weapon

into the wheelhouse with an expression of disgust. "What about the Bren?"

"Nothing left for that either."

Orsini went and pulled the small box of grenades from under the chart table. "At least we've got these."

"If they come close enough," Chavasse said.

Kapo's voice drifted out of the mist again. "It's obvious that you're incapable of moving, Chavasse, but I'll be generous. Give yourself up without any further nonsense and I'll let your friends go free. I give you my word. I'll give you ten minutes to think it over. After that, we'll come and finish you off."

In the silence which followed, Orsini gave an audible grunt and disappeared down the saloon companionway. When he returned, he carried the spare aqualung.

"Help me into this thing quickly," he said to Liri, and turned to Chavasse. "You'll find some more of that plastic explosive in the saloon, Paul, and some chemical detonators. Get them quickly."

"What in hell do you think you're playing at?" Chavasse began, but Orsini gave him an angry shove. "Don't argue. Just do it."

The Italian was buckled into the aqualung and pulling on his rubber flippers when Chavasse came back on deck with the bandolier of explosive.

"I'm going to have a go at fixing Kapo once and for all," Orsini said as he buckled the bandolier around his waist.

Chavasse shook his head. "You haven't got enough time left."

Orsini grinned. "That's what they told me in forty-one when I took a team into Alex. But we got in *and* out and left two British destroyers squatting on their backsides in the mud. I know what I'm doing."

He pulled his mask down, turned from Liri's white face and vaulted over the rail. He had only a rough idea of the direction of the patrol boat, but he knew it couldn't be far away. He swam very fast, kicking strongly with his webbed feet and within a couple of minutes had penetrated the mist.

He surfaced gently and looked about him. There was no sign of the patrol boat, but Kapo's voice boomed over him and he saw a dark outline in the mist.

"Five minutes, Chavasse, that's all."

Orsini went under, swam forward and the keel of the patrol boat loomed out of the water. He worked his way along to the stern, opened the pouches of his bandolier and squeezed handfuls of the plastic explosive between the propeller and the hull. He was fast running out of time and he pushed home the detonator, snapped the end and turned away.

He drove forward, drawing upon his final reserves of strength, feet churning the water into a cauldron and then the hull of the *Buona Esperanza* seemed to be moving towards him and he surfaced.

Chavasse leaned over the rail, Carlo beside him and they hauled him up on to the deck. Somewhere, through the roaring in his ears, the engine of the patrol boat rumbled into life.

When the explosion came, it echoed through the rain and the screams of the dying mingled with it. For a long time, debris continued to fall into the water and then there was silence.

"Holy Mother," Carlo said in awe. "She must have gone down like a stone."

Orsini slowly unbuckled the straps of his aqualung. "How are things below?"

"All finished," Carlo said. "We can move out whenever you're ready."

Liri was kneeling beside Orsini, her cigarette tin open. Chavasse dropped beside them, took one and bent his head to the match as it flared in her hands.

Orsini looked at him curiously. "You're sorry about the girl?"

"Anything she got, she asked for."

Chavasse turned and stood at the rail, aware of the tightness in his throat that couldn't be logically explained, remembering a gay and lovely girl he had met a thousand years ago at an Embassy party in Rome.

His head was aching and he was tired, damned tired and she was calling his name over and over again. He closed his eyes briefly. When he opened them again, she came swimming out of the mist.

She had never looked lovelier, dark hair spreading around her in the water, eyes large in the white face. As she drifted in, she looked up at him appealingly.

"Help me, Paul! Help me!"

He looked down at her, remembering Matt Sorley, Dumont and all the others, good friends who had gone to a hard death because of her.

Orsini said, "For God's sake, Paul. Are we animals?"

Chavasse turned and looked at him and the Italian

shrugged. "If you won't help her, I will."

He started forward and Chavasse shook his head. "My affair, Guilio."

He reached down and pulled Francesca aboard and she sprawled on the deck, coughing and gasping for breath. "Thank you, Paul. You'll never regret it, I promise you."

As she got to her feet, her hand swung up and he was aware of the blade, shining in the harsh morning light. He tried to turn, but he was too late and it caught him in the left side, slicing through flesh, bouncing from the rib cage.

He staggered back, recoiling as much from the cold hatred in her eyes as from the force of the blow and Orsini cried out in dismay. Chavasse was aware of the knife raised high, gleaming in a ray of early morning sunlight which at that moment pierced the mist, and then Liri's voice was lifted in a savage cry.

She moved forward, the heavy automatic Orsini had given her in both hands and one heavy slug after another hammered Francesca back over the rail into the water.

Chavasse was aware of Orsini kneeling beside him, of Liri throwing the gun far out into the sea. He took a deep breath, fighting against the pain.

"I'm all right, Guilio. I'm fine. Just let's get to hell out of here."

Orsini called to Carlo in the wheelhouse and, a moment later, the engines started and the *Buona Esperanza* moved forward slowly.

They passed through a great, widening circle of wreckage from the patrol boat and Liri, standing at the rail, called out sharply and pointed to the water.

Chavasse shook his head, holding his bunched shirt tightly against his side to stem the flow of blood and tried to hear what was being said. There was a roaring in his ears and grey cobwebs seemed to be drifting slowly across his field of vision. He was aware that the engines had stopped, that Carlo had joined her and then Orsini went over the rail.

Chavasse leaned over, suddenly faint, fighting hard against the pain. When he straightened, Carlo was lifting the statue of Our Lady of Scutari over the side.

Orsini brought it across and laid it reverently on the deck in front of Chavasse. "Look, Paul, floating in the wreckage without a mark on her. A miracle."

Carlo went back into the wheelhouse and started the engines and Chavasse sat there looking at the statue. He was crying, which was a strange thing and couldn't be explained and yet somehow the dark serene face smiling up at him seemed to ease his pain.

Above his head, a gull cried sharply, skimmed low over the sea and sped away through the misty rain like a departing spirit.